Play, Pray, and Hooray!

and Fun Activities!

ELIZABETH FRIEDRICH

Illustrated by Ed Koehler

CPH.
SAINT LOUIS

Copyright © 1992, 2002 Concordia Publishing House
Published by Concordia Publishing House, 3558 S. Jefferson Avenue, St. Louis, MO 63118-3968
Manufactured in the United States of America

Originally published as *Close to Jesus,* copyright © 1992 by Concordia Publishing House.

1 2 3 4 5 6 7 8 9 10   11 10 09 08 07 06 05 04 03 02

❋ CONTENTS ❋

SEPTEMBER

Jesus Loves Me 4
I'm Special! 7
Best Friends 10
Here, There, Everywhere 13

OCTOBER

And It Was Good! 16
God Made Me! 19
Look at the Birds and Flowers 22
I Can Make a Difference 27

NOVEMBER

Food for Thousands 30
Praise and Hooray! 33
Thanks Times Ten 36
Count Your Blessings 39

DECEMBER

Promises to Keep 42
Wait for the Lord 45
Happy Birthday, Jesus 48
Shining Stars 53

JANUARY

Growing, Growing... 56
Fabulous Faces 59
God's House 62
Every Part Counts 65

FEBRUARY

Helping Hands 68
Bubbling Love 71
Follow the Leader 74
A Special Book 77

MARCH

Happy Again 80
Hot Line to Heaven 83
Hosanna! Hosanna! 86
Why Good Friday Is Good 89

APRIL

Alleluia! 92
Surprise! Surprise! 95
Noah's Rainy Days 98
A Rainbow Is a Promise 101

MAY

Where Is Jesus? 104
You Are a Gift 107
Silly? Sad? Surprised? 110
Bandages from Heaven 113

JUNE

Little Lambs 116
All Kinds of Families 119
Rejoice! 122
The Greatest Treasure 125

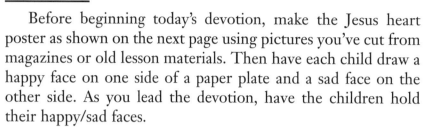

Jesus Loves Me

Bible reference: Mark 10:13–16

PREPARATION ←

Before beginning today's devotion, make the Jesus heart poster as shown on the next page using pictures you've cut from magazines or old lesson materials. Then have each child draw a happy face on one side of a paper plate and a sad face on the other side. As you lead the devotion, have the children hold their happy/sad faces.

Materials Needed

One paper plate for each child

Sheet of poster board or cardboard with a picture of Jesus and a heart

One crayon for each child

DEVOTION

Today we're going to hear a story about Jesus and some children. When the children in the story feel happy, I would like you to show me your happy-face picture. When the children feel sad, show me your sad-face picture.

One day some mothers and fathers told their children, "Today is a special day. Today we're going to see Jesus."

How do you think the children felt? That's right. They were happy. The children knew Jesus was their Friend. They felt so excited they could hardly hold their feet still. And they didn't have to. They walked and ran and jumped and skipped and hopped down the road to see Jesus. Finally they came to the place where Jesus was teaching. Lots of other people crowded around Jesus. The children stood on their tiptoes. But they weren't tall enough. They couldn't see Jesus. How do you think they felt now? That's right. They were sad. The children couldn't wait to be close to Jesus.

The mothers and fathers picked up their children and tried to move closer to Jesus. Now the children could see Him! Jesus looked so kind. How do you think the children felt now? That's right. They felt happy again. The mothers and fathers moved closer and closer to Jesus. The children couldn't wait to give Jesus a big hug.

Just then some men stopped them. "Go away!" the men said. "Don't bother Jesus. He's too busy to see children." How do you

SEPTEMBER

think the children felt now? The children didn't smile now. They felt so sad. They thought they would never get to see Jesus.

Suddenly they heard a special voice. It was Jesus! "Let the children come to Me," He said. "Don't stop them. I love them all so much."

Can you show me how the children felt now? They smiled and laughed and ran to Jesus. He lifted them up into His lap and hugged each of them. Jesus loved each of the children so much. And He loves you too!

Hold up the sheet of poster board with a picture of Jesus and a heart glued to it. Ask one child to come up and stand next to the heart. We can read this picture story together. It says: Jesus loves (child's name). Repeat until each child has had a chance to stand next to the heart as the class "reads" the picture story with you.

Jesus loves *(say the names of all the children in the class).* Can you use your happy and sad faces to show me how that makes you feel? I knew you'd get that right. Jesus' love makes us happy!

Prayer

Dear Jesus, thank You for loving us so much. We know You will always be with us. We know we can always come to You. And that makes us happy! Amen.

Songs

The following songs are from *Little Ones Sing Praise*, CPH.

"Jesus Loves Me, This I Know"

"Happy All the Time"

Jesus Loves Sara

Books to Read

Blessings, Claudia Courtney, CPH, 2000.

Celebrate Feelings, Heidi Bratton, CPH, 2000.

Come to Jesus, Mary Manz Simon, CPH, 1992.

Jesus Makes a Difference, Andy Robb, CPH, 2000.

Jesus Blesses the Children, Gloria Truitt, CPH, 1996.

Stories About Jesus for Little Ones, CPH, 1998.

Why I Love You, God, Michelle Medlock Adams, CPH, 2002.

✱ENRICHMENT ACTIVITIES✱

Shout for Joy Action Rhyme

Stand and clap and shout for joy.
(Stand and clap and shout.)
Jesus loves each girl and boy!
(Hug self.)
Bend and reach and tiptoe too,
(Bend over, then reach arms up and stand on tiptoes.)
Jesus loves both me and you!
(Point to self, then others.)

Jesus Loves Me Bracelet

1. Make one copy of the Jesus picture on page 4 for each child. Give each child an 8½" × 2" strip of paper to decorate with crayons or watercolor markers. Have children paste the Jesus picture on the left end of the strip of paper.

2. Add a heart outline and the child's name so the strip reads "Jesus loves (*child's name*)." Tape or glue the ends to make a bracelet.

Happy Pictures

1. Set out several bright colors of tempera paint in small, shallow dishes.

2. Give children sponges you have cut into various shapes. Clothespins can be clipped to the sponges to make handles. Let the children dip the sponges into the paint and then press them onto heart-shaped paper to make happy pictures.

3. Discuss how the heart-shaped paper reminds us that Jesus loves us, and the bright colors show how happy His love makes us feel.

4. Assemble the completed paintings on a bulletin board under the title "I'm Happy Jesus Loves Me!"

Happy and Sad Faces

Use the happy and sad paper plates from the devotion to start a discussion about what makes us feel happy or sad. To start the discussion, let the children hold their plates and take turns finishing these sentences:

I feel like shouting "Hooray" when …

I feel like crying when …

I dance for joy when …

I frown and whine when …

I'm Special!

Bible references: 1 John 3:2; Luke 12:6

PREPARATION

Materials Needed

Hand mirror

Five different dolls; two boys and three girls if possible

DEVOTION

PART 1

Hold a hand mirror in front of your face as you say the following poem.

Look in the mirror.

Now whom do you see?

It's God's special child.

It's me! It's me!

Let children take turns looking into the mirror. As each child holds the mirror, say the first three lines of the above poem aloud. Then let the child finish the poem by saying the last line aloud.

Part 2

After each child has looked in the mirror and recited the poem, hold up a different doll as you tell the five stories that follow.

This is Molly. Every day she comes running into the classroom. Sometimes she knocks over blocks and toys. She's always in a hurry.

This is J.B. He likes to draw pictures. Some of his pictures are so pretty. Yesterday he drew a picture of a bright red racing car.

This is Sam. Sam loves to run fast. He always wants to wear his white sneakers because he thinks they help him run even faster.

This is Sarah. Sarah can't walk very well. Lots of times she has to ride in a wheelchair. But Sarah is able to move her wheelchair anywhere she wants to go.

This is Amanda. Amanda is so quiet and shy. She loves to play with her dolls. But sometimes she seems afraid of everyone else.

These boys and girls are all different. Some are quiet, some are noisy. Some like to draw, some like to play with dolls. Some can't walk well, some like to run. They are just like us. We're all different too. No two people are exactly alike. But we're all special. We are God's special children. And He loves each one of us so, so much!

Part 3

Now we are going to play the "Guess Who" game. I will begin by saying, "I'm thinking of a special friend who...." *Describe each child in your classroom. For example,* "I'm thinking of a special friend who has a ponytail and blond hair. She is a good helper at school." *Continue until the children correctly guess whom you are describing. Use only positive comments. After the children guess whom you are describing, say,* "(child's name) is God's special child." *Repeat until all children have had a turn to be the "special" one.*

Prayer

Thank You, God! Thank You for *(name each child in your classroom)*. They are all Your special children. Amen.

Songs

"I'm Glad," *The Little Christian's Songbook,* CPH.

The songs listed below are found in *Little Ones Sing Praise,* CPH:

"The Butterfly Song" (Try adding motions to this song.)

"God Made Me"

"I'm Glad"

"Jesus Loves the Little Ones"

Books to Read

God Chose You, Julie Dietrich, CPH, 2000.

I Wonder How God Made Me, Mona

Me Necklace

There's Nobody Just Like Me

Name _____

Gansberg Hodgson, CPH, 1999.

My More-than-Coloring Book About Me, Cathy Spieler, CPH, 1999.

So Big!, Christine Harder Tangvald, CPH, 2001.

So Smart!, Christine Harder Tangvald, CPH 2001.

Tall Body, Short Body, Everybody's Somebody, Mary Hollingsworth, CPH 2000.

Motion Poem

There is nobody just like me.
(Shake head no and point to self.)
I'm as special as can be.
(Hug self.)
Some may dance or jump or run.
(Dance, jump, and run in place.)
Some like dark and some like sun.
(Cover eyes with hand, then point at sun.)
Some are short and some are tall.
(Hold hand low, then high.)
Some like blocks and some like dolls.
(Pretend to build with blocks, then rock doll.)
Some may yell right in the house.
(Cup hands around mouth.)
Some are quiet as a mouse.
(Place index finger over lips.)
But no matter who you see,
(Point at different children.)
There is no one just like me.
(Shake head no and point to self.)

Me Necklace

1. Collect plastic lids from one-pound coffee cans or margarine tubs until you have one for each child in the class. Punch a hole near the top of each lid. Children will thread yarn or string through the hole.

2. Cut circles from construction paper to fit inside the lids. Write each child's name and "There's Nobody Just Like Me" on each circle.

3. Have the children draw a self-portrait or glue a photograph of themselves on the construction paper circle.

4. Have them glue the circles to the inside of the lid, then thread yarn or string through the hole to make a necklace.

Me Shadows

1. Hang a white sheet in a doorway. Shine a light from a flood lamp or projector behind the sheet.

2. Let one child stand, dance, jump, etc., behind the sheet while the rest of the children sit in front of it. Let the children guess what the shadow is doing.

My Special Fingerprints

Use a stamp pad to put each child's fingerprint on a piece of white paper. Examine the unique fingerprints with a magnifying glass. Stress that everyone's fingerprints are different—no two are alike.

Child of the Day

1. Each day or once a week choose one student to be Child of the Day. Use an instant camera to take that child's picture first thing in the morning. Glue the picture to a Me Necklace and let the child wear it all day.

2. As the day progresses, have the child help with classroom duties, share a treasure with the class, and lead the class in various activities. (Be sure to inform the child's parent beforehand so a special treasure can be brought.)

3. Have all the children sit in a circle. Let every student say what he or she likes about the Child of the Day. Only positive, complimentary comments are allowed. Record the comments, and send them and the Me Necklace home with the child.

SEPTEMBER ✳

Best Friends

Bible reference: John 4:1–26

PREPARATION

Use paper strips to cut a paper doll chain.

Materials Needed

One or more strips of paper about 5" × 28". Fold the strip of paper in half, then in half again and again. Draw a simple doll outline as illustrated. Be sure to keep the hands along the folds of paper. Cut along the outline, but do not cut the folds at the hands. When you unfold the dolls, they will be joined at the hands. Cut enough dolls so there is one for every child in the class. Write each child's name on a paper doll. If more than one strip of paper is needed, tape or glue ends together to form one long strip.

Picture of Jesus

Optional:

Red sock   Doll

Smooth rock   Picture of bicycle

Ball

DEVOTION

When I pull on my new red sock,
(Hold up sock.)
Or skip around the entire block,
(Skip in place.)
Or find a smooth and shiny rock—
(Hold up rock.)
My Friend stays right by me.

When I catch a flying ball,
(Throw ball up and catch it.)
Or try to climb a high, high wall,
(Climb in place.)
Or sit and rock my favorite doll—
(Rock doll.)
My Friend stays right by me.

When I ride my two-wheeled bike,

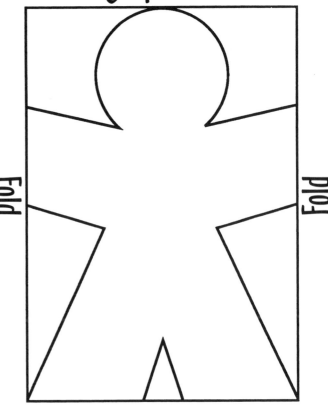

Paper Doll Hang-Ups Pattern

Fold   Fold

(Hold up bike picture.)
Or climb the hills for a long, hard hike,
(Pretend to hike.)
Or do whatever I feel like—
(Outstretch arms.)
My Friend stays right by me.

Do you know who my Friend is? *Hold up picture of Jesus.* It's Jesus! Jesus is my very best Friend. He wants to be your best Friend too.

God's Book, the Bible, tells many stories about Jesus being a Friend to people. One story tells about a day when Jesus walked and walked. He felt tired and thirsty, so He sat down to rest. Just then a woman carrying a jar of water walked up. Jesus asked her, "Will you please give Me a drink?"

The woman looked so surprised. She asked Jesus, "Why are You talking to me? I've done some bad things. Some people won't even talk to me."

Jesus smiled at the woman. "I know you have done some bad things," He said. "But I still love you. And I want to talk to you. I came to be your Savior and your Friend."

Jesus promised to be a Friend to the woman in our story. *Hold up picture of Jesus again.* And Jesus promises to always be our Friend as well. What a wonderful Friend He is!

Jesus also helps us be friends with one another. Jesus, our best Friend, gives us lots of old and new friends at home and at school. Our friends help us and laugh with us and play with us. *Open up paper dolls.* Here at school our friends are … *(say each child's name). Join paper dolls in a circle.* And if we all join hands, we make a circle of boys and girls sharing Jesus' love.

Prayer

Dear Jesus, thank You for all my friends—

Old friends and new friends,
Big friends and little friends,
Tall friends and short friends.
And thank You, Jesus, for always being my best Friend of all. Amen.

Songs

The following songs are from *Little Ones Sing Praise*, CPH:

"Hello, Hello! How Are You?"

"I Have a Friend"

"Jesus, Our Good Friend"

"My Best Friend Is Jesus"

Sing this "piggyback" song from *Little Ones Sing Praise* to the melody "Mary Had a Little Lamb." You might wish to have the children join hands and walk in a circle as you sing.

Will you be a friend of mine,
Friend of mine, friend of mine?
Will you be a friend of mine,
And dance around with me?

My best Friend is Jesus Christ,
Jesus Christ, Jesus Christ.
My best Friend is Jesus Christ.
And He is your Friend too.

Books to Read

In His Footsteps, Cathy Drinkwater Better, CPH, 2000.

Ten Friends Together, Susan Titus Osborn and Christine Harder Tangvald, CPH, 2002.

Why I Love You, God, Michelle Medlock Adams, CPH, 2002.

SEPTEMBER

Paper Doll Hang-Ups

1. On a long table, open the paper doll chain for the devotion.

2. Let each child decorate and personalize the doll with his or her name. Put out yarn, crayons, markers, wallpaper, fabric scraps, paper scraps, ribbon, and other materials you have available.

3. Hang the dolls in the classroom under the heading "Friends of Jesus."

Mirror, Mirror Movement

Let each child choose a partner. Facing the partner, one child makes a movement and the partner copies the movement just like their reflection in a mirror. Encourage children to use different leg, arm, hand movements and expressions.

Sharing Friends

Fill a large pan or large plastic box with sand, salt, or corn meal. Add measuring cups and spoons. Let two children play together, sharing the pan and utensils.

My Favorite Things

1. Cut pictures of items and activities children like from old magazines and catalogs.

2. Give the children long strips of paper and let them choose pictures of their favorite things to glue on the strip.

3. When they are finished, have each child tell the rest of the class about his or her favorite things.

Giggling Friends

Let the children lie on the floor on their backs. Each child should place his or her head on the stomach of another child. Have the children go around the circle with each one saying "Ha!"

Friendly Faces

1. Cut construction paper circles for each child. Have the children make faces on their circles and add yarn hair, button eyes, macaroni noses, and ribbon.

2. Glue a craft stick or tongue depressor to the back of each circle.

3. Fill a tray with play dough and have children press their stick into the dough.

4. Place the tray under a picture of Jesus. Remind the children that Jesus is our best Friend.

Here, There, Everywhere
Bible reference: Mark 4:35–41

PREPARATION ← ▬ ▬ ▬ ▬ ▬ ▬ ▬ ▬ ▬

Materials Needed

Tub filled with water

Small toy boat

DEVOTION

One day Jesus saw a boat floating in the water. *Place boat in tub.* He told His friends, "Let's go to the other side of the lake."

So Jesus and His friends got into the boat. The friends stared to row. But Jesus was very tired, so He went to the back of the boat and fell asleep.

Suddenly a bad storm blew across the lake. *Blow on the water.* Winds howled. The sky turned black. Waves got bigger and bigger. *Use your hand to make "waves" in the tub.*

The friends tried to row the boat, but the waves tossed the boat up and down. Water rushed into the boat. Soon the bottom of the little boat was filled with water. *Make waves bigger and bigger.*

The friends thought they would drown. They shouted to Jesus, "Save us! Save us!"

Jesus woke up and stood up. He spoke to the wind and He spoke to the waves. "Peace! Be still!" Jesus said. *Stop making waves.*

The waves stopped tossing. The wind stopped blowing. The lake was calm again. Jesus looked at His friends. "Don't be afraid," He told them. "I will always be with you. I will always help you."

Jesus helped His friends when they were afraid. He promised He would always be with them. Jesus will always be with you too. When you're sleeping or playing or riding in the car or at home or at school, Jesus is always with

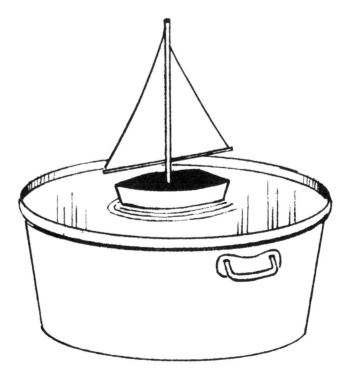

you. He will always help you. He's here. *Point around room.* He's there. *Point outside room.* He's everywhere. *Make a big circle with your arm.*

I'm going to name different times you might feel afraid just like Jesus' friends did in the story I told you. After each afraid time, I'll stop and let you tell me the name of someone who will always be with you. Who is always there? That's right. Jesus is always with us.

When the buzzing bee comes so near to me,
Someone is there! It's … (Jesus!)
When a big blue ball makes me start to fall,
Someone is there! It's … (Jesus!)
When there is no light and I'm scared at night,
Someone is there! It's … (Jesus!)
When my swing flies high up into the sky,
Someone is there! It's … (Jesus!)
When the spider crawls right up my walls,
Someone is there! It's … (Jesus!)
When thunder crashes and lighting flashes,
Someone is there! It's … (Jesus!)

Jesus is with us wherever we are. He's here. *Point around room.* He's there. *Point outside room.* He's everywhere. *Make a big circle with your arm.*

Sing the piggyback song "Where Is Jesus?" from Little Ones Sing Praise *to the melody "Are You Sleeping?"*

Where is Jesus? Where is Jesus?
Here He is! Here He is.
With me on the playground, with me on the playground.
Yes, He is, Yes, He is.

Ask the children to think of other lines to sing in place of "With me on the playground." Sing your new stanzas together.

Prayer

When my tummy aches,
(Hold stomach.)
And my two legs shake,
(Wiggle legs.)
Stay with me, Jesus.
(Hug self.)

Near a buzzing bee,
(Move hand back and forth.)
If I hurt my knee,
(Rub knee.)
Stay with me, Jesus.
(Hug self.)

In the dark of night,
(Cover eyes with hand.)
When the sun is bright,
(Shade eyes with hand.)
Stay with me, Jesus.
(Hug self.)

When I'm scared or sad,
(Pretend to wipe tears.)
Happy, good, or bad,
(Smile, then frown and shake finger.)
Stay with me, Jesus.
(Hug self.)

Song

"He's Got the Whole World in His Hands," *Little Ones Sing Praise*, CPH. Consider using these simple hand motions to accompany the song:

Hands (Cup palms together.)
Whole world (Bend fingers to form a ball.)
Wind (Wave arms from side to side.)
Rain (Wiggle fingers while lowering arms.)
Sun (Point at sky with left hand.)
Moon (Point at sky with right hand.)

SEPTEMBER

Tiny little baby (*Rock arms back and forth.*)
Both you and me (*Point first at someone else, then at self.*)

Books to Read

I Wonder How God Hears Me, Mona Gansberg Hodgson, CPH 1999.

Jesus Makes a Difference, Andy Robb, CPH, 2000.

My B-I-B-L-E, Cathy Drinkwater Better, CPH, 1999.

Ten Friends Together, Susan Titus Osborn and Christine Harder Tangvald, CPH, 2002.

ENRICHMENT ACTIVITIES

In the Boat

Place masking tape on the floor or rug to outline a rowboat. Let the children sit inside the "boat" and act out the Bible story.

Storm in a bottle

1. Fill a two-liter plastic bottle about half full with water.
2. Add enough blue food coloring to turn water deep blue.
3. Drop into the bottle a small wooden spool, short twig, or small toy boat that will float. Screw the lid on tightly.
4. Let the children take turns tipping the bottle back and forth to make waves and toss the boat in the water.

Windy Pictures

Mix tempera paint to a runny consistency. Let each child drip some paint to make a puddle on a sheet of paper, and then use straws to blow the paint around the paper.

Paper-Bag Kites

1. Give one paper lunch bag to each child and let him or her decorate the bottom half of each side with crayons or markers.
2. Open the bag so the bottom is flat, and fold down the top several times.
3. Glue or staple crepe paper streamers to the fold around the top of the bag.
4. Punch two holes in opposite sides of the bottom fold of the bag and tie on yarn.
5. Let the children take their kites outside. Watch the wind lift and toss the kites as the children run and play.

And It Was Good!

PREPARATION

Gather materials in advance. When you get ready for the devotion, assemble the children. As you lead the devotion, glue, tape, or staple the paper cutouts and pictures to the butcher paper to make a mural.

Materials Needed

Large sheet of butcher paper tacked on the wall or laid flat on the floor

Construction paper cutouts:	Darker blue in shape of lakes
One sheet black and white	Brown for hills
Light blue for sky	Green for grass
White for clouds	Yellow for sun and moon

Pictures cut from magazines or catalogs: trees, flowers, fish, birds, animals, a man, and a woman

Gold or silver foil star stickers

DEVOTION

A long, long time ago there was no world. Only God was there. All was dark, just like this. *Hold up black paper.* Then God said, "Let there be light." And there was light! *Hold up white paper.* God made the night, and God made the day. And it was good!

The next day God said, "Let there be a sky." As soon as God said it, a bright blue sky appeared. *Place blue sky on the butcher paper.* And it was good!

The third day God put water into lakes and ponds and oceans and clouds. *Place blue water and white clouds on the butcher paper.* He made high hills. *Place brown hills.* Then God said, "Let plants grow on the dry land." Right away bushes and trees and grass and flowers grew. *Place green grass and plant pictures.* And it was good!

The fourth day God said, "Let lights shine in the sky." *Place yellow sun and moon.* Sunshine warmed the world by day, and the moon shone at night. Something else lit the sky at night—beautiful twinkling stars. *Let each child place a star sticker on the paper.* And it was good!

The next day God worked again. He said, "Let fish fill the water. Let birds fill the air." *Place pictures of fish in the blue lakes and*

pictures of birds in the sky. And it was good!

On the sixth day God made the animals. He made … *name each animal as you place its picture on the mural.* Animals of all sizes and shapes lived in God's wonderful world. Last of all, God made a man and a woman. *Place man and woman pictures.*

God looked at the beautiful world He had made. He was pleased. God said, "It is good! It is very, very good!"

Prayer

My nose loves to smell the flowers so sweet.
(Touch nose.)
My mouth loves to taste all the foods I eat.
(Touch mouth.)
My ears always hear a whisper or yell.
(Touch ears.)
And red, green, or blue—my eyes always tell.
(Touch eyes.)
I love warm puppies so soft to my touch.
(Pretend to pat puppy.)
Thanks, God, for a world I enjoy so much!
(Clap hands.)

Songs

The following songs are from *Little Ones Sing Praise*, CPH:
"My God Is So Great"
"Oh, Who Can Make a Flower?"
"Thank You for the World So Sweet"
"Thank You, Loving Father"
"Who Made the Sky So Bright and Blue?"

Books to Read

I Wonder Who Hung the Moon in the Sky, Mona Gansberg Hodgson, CPH, 1999.

My More-than-Coloring Book About Creation, Cathy Spieler, CPH, 1999.

The Upside-Down, Inside-Out, Backwards, Oopsy-Daisy Book, Mary Hollingsworth, CPH, 2000.

What Next? Mary Manz Simon, CPH, 1990.

Who Made the World?, Andy Robb, CPH, 1999.

OCTOBER

Nature Games

Color Hunt. Take the class outside and have them stand in one place. Ask children to identify colors they can see from that one spot. Move to another place and repeat.

Sounds Around. Have children sit outside in a circle, as far away from street and school noises as possible, and tell them to be very quiet. Ask them to raise one finger each time they hear a sound from nature—a bird singing, wind rushing, water dripping, leaves crunching, etc.

Nature Walk

Lead the children on a nature walk. Observe natural wonders in your environment. Study the intricacies of a spider's web, watch a worm crawling on the sidewalk, feel the rough texture of tree bark, or count blades of grass. Let the children feel your own excitement and awe in God's beautiful world.

Bring two bags along on your walk—one for trash and one for treasures. Fill the trash bag with any litter you find. Collect rocks, leaves, fallen twigs, and other items in the treasure bag to bring back to class. Be sure not to pick things that are growing (flowers or other plants) or otherwise harm any of the wonders you find. Use items from the treasure bag to make a creation collage.

And It Was Good!

Collect pictures of the items named in the following litany. Give the pictures to the children. Ask them to hold their pictures high when items are named. Repeat until all children have held up a picture.

Teacher: God made red flowers.
God made tall trees.
He even made the buzzing bee.
Children: And it was good!
Teacher: God made cool water.
God made blue sky.
He even made the birds that fly.
Children: And it was good!
Teacher: God made soft puppies.
God made bright sun.
He even made ponies the run.
Children: And it was good!
Teacher: God made people
God made you and me.
He made us part of His family.
Children: And it was good!

Around the World Paintings

1. Set out three or more colors of tempera paint and let the children paint circles on paper to represent the world God made.

2. Display the paintings on a bulletin board under the title "And It Was Good!"

OCTOBER

<table>
<tr><td>

God Made Me!

</td><td>

Bible references: Psalm 139:13–16
Genesis 1:27

</td></tr>
</table>

PREPARATION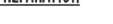

Materials Needed

Flannel board

Felt or heavy paper and Velcro or sandpaper

Cut body parts from heavy paper or felt. You will need a head, a body, arms, legs, feet, hands, eyes, ears, a mouth, and a nose. If you use paper, attach Velcro or sandpaper to the back of these pieces so they can be used on a flannel board.

DEVOTION

Our bodies can do so many wonderful things. We can see the stars in the sky and hear the birds sing. We can touch soft blankets and taste spicy pizza. We can run and dance and jump.

God made our bodies. He fit everything together just perfectly. Our fingers come together to pick things up. *Pick something up with fingers.* Our eyes move all around so we can see many things. *Move eyes up and down.* Our knees bend to help us walk and run. *Bend knees, take a few steps.*

Inside our bodies, God gave us lungs to breath air. *Take a deep breath.* He gave us a heart to pump blood all through our bodies. *Feel heartbeat at pulse in the neck.* He built our bones to make our bodies strong. *Feel bones in the hand.* God thought of everything when He made us.

I have some pieces for the flannel board that show the parts of our wonderful bodies. *Pass out the pieces to the children.* We're going to put all these parts of our bodies together to make a person. Who has the head? Where does the head belong on the body? *Have that child come up and place the head at the top of the flannel board. Continue in this manner until all body parts are assembled.*

Ask the children to close their eyes while you move one part of the body to the wrong position. For example, switch an eye with the nose or place both ears on the same side of the head. Then have children open their eyes. Which part of the body is in the wrong place? Can you put it back where God made it? *Let one child place the body part back in its correct position. Continue switching body parts as long as children remain interested.*

Lead the children in the following motion poem.

Eyes and ears and mouth and nose,

OCTOBER

Hands and hair and legs and toes.
Point to each body part as it is named.
God *(point upward)* made every part you see *(point to eyes).*
Head *(touch head)* to toe *(point at toes),*
He's proud of me *(hug self).*

Prayer

Ask the children to point to each body part as you name it in the prayer.

Thank You, God, for making my wonderful body. Thank You for my hands, shoulders, forehead, legs, head, fingers, knees, feet, ankles, elbows, toes, wrists, mouth, waist, neck, cheeks, heels, chin, eyes, and nose. Amen.

Songs

The following songs are from *Little Ones Sing Praise*, CPH:
"God Made Me, Every Part You See"
"I Can Stamp"
"My Hands and Feet"

Books to Read

The Grand Plan, Claudia Courtney, CPH, 2000.

I Wonder How God Made Me, Mona Gansberg Hodgson, CPH, 1999.

My More-than-Coloring Book About Me, Cathy Spieler, CPH, 1999.

Tall Body, Short Body, Everybody's Somebody, Mary Hollingsworth, CPH, 2000.

Whose Nose? Whose Toes?, Debbie Reinertson, CPH, 1999.

Number Man

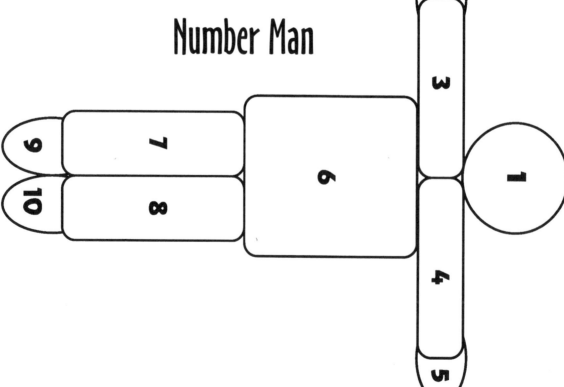

Who Am I? Bulletin Board

1. Let the children draw pictures of themselves. If you wish, let them add button eyes, fabric clothing, and yarn hair.

2. Assemble the pictures on the bulletin board under the words "Who Am I?" At the bottom of the bulletin board place these words: "I Am God's Creation."

Cookie Children

1. Mix a batch of dough for sugar cookies. Chill until ready to use. You can also use packaged dough from the supermarket.

2. Give each child a small ball of dough to shape into a head, a medium sized ball to roll into a body, and a larger ball to roll into legs and arms. Press the dough flat on a cookie sheet. Bake as directed.

3. After the cookies are cool, let the children mix icing to decorate their cookie children.

Nose to Knee

Lead the children in a game of body awareness as they touch body parts with other body parts:

Touch your nose to knee

Chin to chest

Hand to elbow

Ear to shoulder

Foot to knee

Hand to shoulder

Elbow to knee

Wrist to cheek

Hand to waist

Finger to forehead

Heel to toe

Number Man

1. Draw a large number man as shown on page 20 on a sheet of butcher paper. Tape to the floor.

2. Have each child throw a beanbag onto the number man and name the numeral where the bag lands. For example, if the beanbag lands on the numeral three, the child calls out "three."

Mirror Painting

Let each child use shaving cream to finger-paint his or her reflection on a large mirror. If available, a full-length mirror is ideal for this activity. Wipe the mirror clean after each child has painted.

God Made Me Activities

Set up a learning center where the children can use the bodies God gave them. Suggested activities include skipping, hopping on both feet, hopping on one foot, catching a ball or beanbag, rolling a ball to a partner, and walking along a line or balance beam.

An Inside View

Assemble as many of the following items as possible, or others you can think of, to give the children a better understanding of the wonders inside their bodies: Models of the human body, old x-rays, impressions of teeth from a dentist or orthodontist, stethoscope, microscope with slides showing cells and strands of hair.

OCTOBER

Look at the Birds and Flowers	Bible reference: Matthew 6:25–34

PREPARATION ← — — — — — — — — — —

Materials Needed

Completely white paper flower, including white stem

Picture of a field of flowers in full bloom, a collage of pictures of brightly colored flowers cut from catalogs, or a vase filled with fresh flowers

A bird—use a figurine, picture, paper cutout, or whatever is available

Pictures of an elephant, sea gull, squirrel, fish, and snail

DEVOTION

Part 1

Hold up white paper flower. I brought a flower with me today. Does this look like a real flower? Why not? That's right. This paper flower is *all* white. It has no color at all. Even the stem is white. Real flowers come in lots of colors—like this. *Show picture, collage, or bouquet of flowers.*

What colors do you see in these flowers? *Let children name the colors.* The flowers don't make their own bright colors. God does. God made all these flowers and dressed them in bright colors. He made red flowers and yellow flowers and purple flowers. He made orange flowers and pink flowers and blue flowers. Jesus said that even the richest king in the whole world never had clothes as beautiful as the flowers. God gives them just what they need.

Hold up bird. Birds like this fly high in the sky. Does he work hard to plant his food? Does he gather his food into the barn? No, he doesn't worry at all about his food. When he feels hungry, he finds some seeds or bugs to eat. God gives him all the food he needs.

God must love His world very much. He dresses the flowers in beautiful colors. He gives the birds food to eat. If God takes such good care of the flowers and birds, we know He will take good care of us. Because we are His own children, God loves us more than anything. He even sent Jesus to die for our sins and save us. We can be sure He will give us food and clothes—and everything else we need!

Part 2

Read the poem below to the children. Hold up the appropriate animal picture as you read each verse.

God gave the elephant skin so thick
It feels just like a wall.
Wouldn't you laugh if an elephant
Wore a coat when he came to call?

The seagull has feathers soft and smooth
So he can fly above.
How would he know just where to go
If he dressed in mittens or gloves?

God blessed the squirrel with plenty of fur
To warm her winter nights.
What would you think if you saw her one day
Wearing a long pair of tights?

Scales on the fish make the water slide
Smoothly as he swims by.
Would he be late if he had to wait
To put on a hat and tie?

God gave the snail a shell to serve
As his house and his retreat.
How could he manage to hide inside
With great big boots on his feet?

God thought of every living thing—
Animals don't need clothes,
Because God's already protected them,
From their tops down to their toes!

If God takes such good care of His animals, then He surely will care for us, His children! Can you name some ways God cares for us? *Let the children give examples.* Let's thank God for His care!

Prayer

Dear God, the flowers and birds and animals all remind us of Your care for the world You made. Thank You for taking such good care of us! We love You, God. Amen.

Songs

The following songs are from *Little Ones Sing Praise*, CPH:

"God's a Father Kind and True"

"The Lord Is Good to Me"

"Thank You for the World So Sweet"

23

Flying Birds Pattern

FOLD

FOLD

OCTOBER ✱

Flower Arranging and Rearranging

Secure Styrofoam or clay in the bottom of a basket. Provide plastic or silk flowers and have the children arrange and rearrange the flowers in the basket.

Bird Feeders

Have the children make bird feeders. Here are several simple suggestions:

- Tie string or yarn to the top of pinecones. Cover pinecones with peanut butter and birdseed. Hang outside.

- Thread "o"-shaped cereal onto string or yarn. (First dip the end of the string into white glue and let it harden to make threading easier.)

- Fill dried orange rinds with birdseed. Poke three holes in the rind, thread long pieces of string or yarn through the holes, tie string at the top, and hang outdoors.

Musical Birds and Flowers

Play a classical music selection that features different tempos. Let the children pretend to be birds flying through the air in time to the music. Let them pretend to be flowers growing and swaying to the music.

Rhyme Time

As you read the following verses to the children, leave off the last word. Let the children suggest a rhyming word to finish the verse.

Watch the birds flying so high.
God put them up in the … (sky).
Flowers grow from just one seed.
God gives them each thing they …
(need).
Milk and bread and even meat.
God gives us good food to … (eat).
Shoes and socks so fresh and new.
God will always care for … (you).
Food to eat and clothes to wear.
We know God will always … (care).

Flying Birds

1. Cut out birds like the one illustrated on the previous pages.

2. Set out one or two colors of tempera paint and let children use feathers instead of brushes to paint their birds.

3. After the paint has dried, let the children glue feathers onto their birds.

4. Fold the birds at the bottom, attach string to the center inside of the fold, and hang from the ceiling. Let the birds "fly" freely.

OCTOBER

I Can Make a Difference

PREPARATION

Materials Needed

Puppet	Piece of paper
Candy wrapper	Six-pack ring that held aluminum cans
Trashcan	Scissors
Toothbrush	Empty aluminum can

DEVOTION

(The puppet, Theodore, enters, pretending to eat a candy bar and carrying the wrapper in his hand.)

Theodore: Yum … yum … yum … yum! This is the best candy bar I've ever tasted. I'm all done now. I don't need this anymore. *(Throws candy wrapper on the floor.)*

Teacher: Theodore, look what you just did!

Theodore: *(Looks around)* I don't see anything. What did I do?

Teacher: You threw your candy wrapper on the floor. It belongs in the trashcan.

Theodore: Oops. I forgot. *(Picks up wrapper and puts it in the trash can.)* There! Is that better?

Teacher: Much better. Thank you, Theodore.

Theodore: I'm going to brush my teeth now. I don't want any cavities. *(Picks up the toothbrush and pretends to turn on water.)* I need some water. *(Begins brushing teeth.)*

Teacher: Theodore, why are you letting the water run and run? That wastes a lot of water. If you just turn the water on to wet and rinse your brush, you'll use much less.

Theodore: I never thought of that. I guess it's worth a try.

Teacher: It surely is, Theodore. Picking up trash and not wasting water when we brush our teeth are just two of the things we can do to help take care of God's world.

Theodore: You mean there are more?

Help Keep God's World Clean

OCTOBER

Teacher: Lots more. *(Hold up sheet of paper.)* We can draw on both sides of our paper instead of just one side. *(Hold up six-pack ring and snip rings with scissors.)* We can ask Mom or Dad to help us use a scissors to snip the circles on these six-pack rings so birds, fish, and other animals don't get caught in them. We can crush aluminum cans with our feet and save them for the recycling center. That way they can be used again. *(Crush can with foot.)*

Theodore: Wow! I can make a difference! I can do all those things to help take care of God's world.

Teacher: All those things and even more, Theodore. God made such a beautiful world for us to live in. But it's up to us to keep it clean and to care for all of God's creations.

Prayer

Dear God, we love the world You made for us. It's our home. Help us to take care of Your world. Amen.

Songs

"This Is the Day," *Little Ones Sing Praise*, CPH.

Try singing this "piggyback" song from *Little Ones Sing Praise* to the melody "Are You Sleeping?"

It's a new day, it's a new day,
Given by God, given by God.
Join the celebration, join the celebration!
Sing His praise! Sing His praise!

Counting Rhyme

Hold up another finger each time you say a number.

One, two …
It's up to you.
Three, four …
We can do more.
Five, six …
God's world to fix.
Seven, eight …
It's not too late.
Nine, ten …
I know I can!

Adopt a Tree

Choose a tree nearby to adopt. If possible, plant your own tree. Let the children visit the adopted tree on a regular basis and plan activities around it:

- Have a picnic next to or under the tree.
- Take leaf and bark rubbings of the tree.
- Draw pictures of the tree in different seasons.
- Make sure the tree is watered and mulched.
- Decorate the tree.

Recycled Milk Carton Blocks

1. Cut the tops off clean cardboard milk cartons.
2. Put two cartons together to make large blocks for the classroom.
3. Use the blocks to build walls or buildings to act out Bible stories.

Litterbags

1. Let the children make litterbags for their family's car. Fold down the tops of brown paper lunch bags several times.
2. Punch holes in the sides and attach a yarn handle.
3. Fold bags flat and let the children paint or decorate their bags with watercolor markers.
4. Write "Help keep God's world clean" on each bag.

Classroom Conservation

Try some of these ideas to help the children in your classroom develop an attitude of conservation:

- Ask each child to bring a reusable plastic cup to school for juice at snack time. Use these cups in place of paper cups.
- Keep a container on the shelf for paper left over after art activities. Show the children how to place their scraps into the container to save for future uses.
- Ask parents to help their children collect items that can be reused in the classroom: egg cartons, plastic margarine tubs, baby food jars, magazines, envelopes, Styrofoam trays, fabric and yarn scraps, milk cartons, Styrofoam bits, berry baskets, old cards, and spools are just a few reusable items.

Recycled Art

1. Set out a collection of recycled materials that can be used for art activities. Include the items suggested above.
2. Let the children use the materials to make collages or creative constructions.
3. Use glue and tape to assemble the creations.

OCTOBER

Food for Thousands

Bible references: Matthew 14:13–21; Mark 6:30–44; Luke 9:10–17; John 6:1–13

PREPARATION

Materials Needed

Grocery bag filled with empty food boxes, cartons, and cans, including a milk carton, cereal box, and egg carton

DEVOTION

Last night I was so-o-o hungry. I looked in my refrigerator, but it was almost empty. I checked my cupboards, but they were empty too. Can anyone guess where I went to find some food? That's right, I went to the grocery store. *Show children the filled grocery bag.* And this is what I came home with. *Unpack the bag and name the items inside.*

Whenever we are hungry, we know we can find food at the grocery store. But one day when Jesus was preaching to lots and lots of people, the people got hungry, and Jesus' disciples didn't know where to get food. Follow my motions to see what happened. *This is based on John 6:1–13.*

One day many people came to hear Jesus preach.
(Extend arms out.)
They listened and listened. He had so much to teach.
(Cup hands around ears.)
The day passed by quickly. The sun set in the sky.
(Move arm in arc from left to right.)
"We're hungry and can't find food," the people did cry.
(Rub stomach.)
One boy said, "I have two fish and five loaves of bread."
(Hold up two fingers on one hand and five on the other.)
Jesus looked up to heaven. "Thank You, God," He said.
(Fold hands and look up.)
There was plenty of food for all—both rich and poor.
(Nod head yes.)
They never ran out 'cause Jesus always made more.
(Shake head no.)
When they were finished, Jesus said, "Pick up the scraps."
(Bend over and pretend to put food scraps into basket.)
The people were so full, they felt ready for naps.
(Lay head on hands.)

NOVEMBER

After starting with two fish and five loaves of bread,
(Hold up two fingers on one hand and five on the other.)
Helpers picked up 12 basketfuls—and everyone was fed.
(First hold up two fingers, then hold up all ten fingers.)

Jesus made one little boy's lunch grow into enough food to feed lots of people. And when everyone was full, they still had 12 baskets full of leftovers! Jesus took such good care of all those people. And He takes good care of us too. *Show grocery items again.* He gives us all these foods to eat.

Hold up egg carton. God made the chickens that give us eggs. *Hold up milk carton.* God made the cows that give us milk. *Hold cereal box.* God made the grain that we eat in this cereal. *Continue in this manner, tracing other items in your grocery bag to God. Help* children understand the relationship between God and His gift of food to us.

God is so good to us. Let's thank Him for our food. *See prayer below.*

Prayer

Give each child one of the empty food containers to hold. At the appropriate time in the prayer, each child will thank God for that food. As you lead the prayer, move around the room and gently touch children on the shoulder when it is their turn to thank God for the food item they are holding. Help any children who are shy about naming their food items.

Dear God, You are so good to us. Thank You for giving us our food. Thank You for_____. Amen.

Songs

Any of these songs from *Little Ones Sing Praise* (CPH), can be used as prayers before

God's Garden Bulletin Board

snack time. They can be sung or spoken.
"The Lord Is Good to Me"
"Our Hands We Fold"
"Thank You for the World So Sweet"

Books to Read

Little Is Big, Claudia Courtney, CPH, 1999.

Rumble, Rumble, Mary Manz Simon, CPH, 1990.

Stories About Jesus for Little Ones, CPH, 1998.

Toddlers' Action Bible, Robin Currie, CPH, 1998.

What's for Lunch?, Joanne Bader, CPH, 1997.

ENRICHMENT ACTIVITIES

Food Baskets

Place an empty basket in the center of the table. Have children cut or tear pictures of food from magazines. Remind them that God gives us everything we have. Fill the basket with the pictures.

Place another larger empty basket in one corner of the room. Encourage the children to bring in nonperishable food items to fill the basket for donation to a local food pantry.

Place Mats

1. Write these words on strips of construction paper: "Give thanks to the LORD" (Psalm 106:1). Give one strip to each child.

2. Give each child a large sheet of construction paper in a contrasting color.

3. Let the children paste both the Bible verse strip and the pictures from the food basket activity onto the sheet of construction paper.

4. Laminate the place mats for use at snack time.

Fruit and Vegetable Match-up

1. Cut matching pictures of various fruits and vegetables from seed catalogs.

2. Glue one set of fruits and vegetables onto squares of cardboard. Glue the other set onto index cards and trim to fit the pictures.

3. Let the children match the fruits and vegetables.

Lunch to Munch

Let the children make their own lunch or snack. To make "funny face" sandwiches, have children spread peanut butter on bread and add coconut hair, raisin eyes and nose, and a carrot stick mouth.

For dessert, shake up a batch of instant pudding. First mix the milk and pudding in a large bowl. Then divide the pudding mixture into small baby food jars, tighten the lids, and let the children shake the jars until pudding is thickened.

God's Garden Bulletin Board

Prepare a bulletin board as illustrated on page 31. Cut ears of corn, apples, potatoes, tomatoes, peanuts, carrots, and pumpkins from construction paper.

Discuss the fruits and vegetables. Attach each fruit and vegetable to the appropriate spot on the bulletin board (potatoes, peanuts, and carrots underground; tomatoes on a plant; pumpkins on vines; apples on trees; and corn on stalks).

Praise and Hooray!

Bible references:
1 Samuel 16; Psalms 8, 27, 63, 145

PREPARATION

Materials Needed

Bible

Simple crayon or watercolor marker illustrations of these psalms:

Psalm 8—outline of the world with sketches of the moon, stars, birds, fish, and sheep

Psalm 27—light bulb

Psalm 63—outline of lips and hands

Psalm 145—outline of a large heart

DEVOTION

David was a shepherd boy. Every morning he led his sheep to fields of sweet green grass. He helped his sheep find cool water to drink. Sometimes, when a bear or lion would come near, David scared them away and kept his sheep safe.

But much of the time David sat under a shady tree and just watched. He watched his sheep quietly eating grass. He laughed as the baby lambs jumped over one another and raced around their mothers. He saw birds flying and worms wriggling and spiders weaving webs. He felt the sun move across the sky, and he discovered shapes in the white clouds.

David felt so happy. God had made such a wonderful world!

David wanted to thank God for His world … and His care … and His love. So David picked up his harp and sang. How David loved to sing! He loved to make up songs to thank and praise God.

David sang songs like this:

Hold up the Psalm 8 picture.

What a wonderful world You have made, Lord!

You made the moon and stars.

You made the birds in the sky and the fish in the sea.

You made the sheep that graze in the fields.

You made me!

Thank You, Lord, for Your wonderful world.

Hold up the Psalm 27 picture.

The Lord is my Light and my salvation.

I will not be afraid.

My God will keep me safe.

33

Hold up the Psalm 63 picture.
God's love is better than anything.
My lips will praise Him.
My hands will praise Him.
I will praise Him all day and all night.
I will sing and praise God forever and ever.

Hold up the Psalm 145 picture.
I will praise Your name forever and ever, O God.
I will celebrate and sing about Your love.
I will think of Your wonderful works.
I will tell of Your great deeds.
Joyfully sing to the Lord!

David wrote many songs to God. We are able to read David's songs in the Bible. *Hold up Bible.* David's songs are called psalms.

Prayer

Let the children compose their own psalm of praise to God. Ask them to suggest things they would like to praise God for. Write out their suggestions. Put their suggestions together into a simple litany where the children respond to each suggestion with the same simple words.

Songs

Sing any and all praise songs the children already know. This is a wonderful time to sing praises to God and then sing some more! You might wish to incorporate some of the enrichment activities suggested for this unit in your praise celebrations.

"Hallelujah! Praise Ye the Lord!" *Little Ones Sing Praise,* CPH.

"I Have the Joy," *Little Ones Sing Praise,* CPH.

"Making Melody in My Heart," *Little Ones Sing Praise,* CPH.

"Praise Him, Praise Him," *Little Ones Sing Praise,* CPH.

"Sing, David, Sing," *The Little Christian's Songbook,* CPH.

Books to Read

Praise Prayers, James S. Yagow, CPH, 1999.

Psalms for Kids, Robert Baden, CPH, 2001.

Weather Windows: Autumn, Wendy Maas, CPH, 2001.

Why I Love You, God, Michelle Medlock Adams, CPH, 2002.

Creative Dancing

Play a variety of music selections. Let the children make up movements to go with the music. Explain that someone praised God by writing the music, someone else praised God by playing the music, and now they praise God by moving to the beautiful sounds.

Kitchen Orchestra

Make simple rhythm instruments to accompany your praise celebrations, such as:

- Oatmeal box or coffee can with plastic lid as a drum
- Pan lids to crash together for cymbals
- Wooden spoons as rhythm sticks
- Bunch of keys as a shaker
- Spoon scraped across a cake cooling rack as a harp

Crayon Dancing

1. Place a very large sheet of butcher paper on the floor.
2. Set out crayons at different places on the paper for the children to use.
3. Play several short musical selections.
4. Let the children gather around the paper and make the crayons "dance" on the paper in time to the music.

Cheers and Claps

Let the children clap in rhythm to these cheers:
God is great.
God is grand.
Let's give Him a great big hand.

Sing, sing, sing.
Let our praises ring.
To our God and King.

Hooray! Hooray!
God is here with us today!

Praise Pennants

1. Have the children paint on pennant-shaped paper.
2. When the paint has dried, write praise words, such as "God Is Great" or "Praise the Lord" on each pennant.
3. Tape drinking straws to small pennants and paper towel tubes or tightly rolled newspaper to larger pennants to make handles.
4. Use them in your praise celebrations.

NOVEMBER

DEVOTION

Ask children to hold up their hands and move their fingers like you do. One time long ago, 10 sick men stood by the side of the road. *Hold up all 10 fingers.*

They waited and waited and waited for Jesus. *Let fingers droop.*

Finally, they saw Jesus coming. *Hold fingers up straight.*

They shouted, "Jesus, please make us well." *Wiggle fingers.*

Jesus told the men to go to the church in the village. So the 10 sick men started walking. *Move hands back and forth with fingers outstretched.*

On the way they looked at their hands and arms and legs and faces. *Hold hands with palms facing together. Bend fingers at different times like men looking at each other.* They were well!

The men were so happy as they hurried into the village. *Move hands quickly back and forth with fingers outstretched.*

But one man stopped. *Hold up only one index finger.* He turned around. He hurried back down the road to Jesus. *Hop index finger.* He kneeled down and thanked Jesus for making him well. *Bend index finger.*

How many sick men stood by the side of the road? Let's count them. *Hold up all 10 fingers and count them.* How many men came to thank Jesus? *Hold up one index finger.* That's right. Only one. Was Jesus happy when the one man thanked Him? Yes, of course He was. He was very happy that one man came back to thank Him.

But Jesus made 10 men well. *Hold up all 10 fingers.* Let's count them again. *Count fingers.* All 10 men could dance. *Wiggle fingers.* All 10 men could jump. *Bend fingers up and down.* All 10 men could run. *Move hands quickly back and forth with fingers outstretched.* How happy Jesus would have been if all 10 men had remembered to thank Him! *Clap hands together.*

Prayer

Now let's fold our fingers and thank Jesus for some of the wonderful things He has done for us.

Thank You, Jesus, for eyes to see, ears to hear, hands to touch, noses to smell, and mouths to taste. Thank You for fingers to wiggle, feet to walk, and hands to hold. Thank You, Jesus

Touch Collage

"Thank You, God for fingers to touch."

for my wonderful body. Thank You for keeping me well. Amen.

Songs

The following songs are from *Little Ones Sing Praise*, CPH:

"God Is So Good"

"It's Good to Give Thanks"

"The Lord Is Good to Me"

"Thank You for the World So Sweet"

"Thank You, Loving Father"

Sing the following song to the melody "Three Blind Mice":

Ten sick men,

Ten sick men. *(Hold up 10 outstretched fingers.)*

Jesus made them well.

Jesus made them well.

But only one came back to say, (Hold up

one finger.)

"Thank You, Jesus, this special day.

Only You could heal me this way."

Ten well men,

Ten well men. (Hold up 10 outstretched fingers.)

Books to Read

Thank You Jesus, Mary Manz Simon, CPH, 1994.

I Wonder What Can I Give God, Mona Gansberg Hodgson, CPH, 1999.

He Remembered to Say Thank You, Victor Naum, CPH, 1975

Color Mixing

1. Fill a clear plastic one- or two-liter bottle with water. Gather the children around the bottle. Put a few drops of blue food coloring into the water.

2. Let the children watch the color float down the water. As the color spreads, add a few drops of red food coloring to the water to make purple. Ask the children to identify each color as it appears.

3. Refill the bottle with clean water and repeat with yellow and blue to make green. Refill once again and repeat with red and yellow to make orange.

Sound Shakers

1. Fill old film containers or margarine tubs with items that make different sounds when you shake them. You might include salt, rice, popcorn, flour, oatmeal, and miniature marshmallows.

2. Prepare two of each. Let the children shake the containers and try to match the ones that sound alike.

Goop

Make a batch of "goop" and let the children experience the tactile sensations it produces: Mix 3 tablespoons cornstarch and 2 tablespoons cold water.

Squeeze it, and it crumbles and feels dry. Hold it in a relaxed hand, and it drips and oozes through fingers.

Touch Collages

1. Let the children assemble collages using items with different textures. Include sandpaper, cotton balls, feathers, fabric scraps, buttons, twisted pasta, pebbles, etc.

2. Write these words on each child's collage: "Thank You, God, for fingers to touch." (See page 37.)

3. Encourage the children to close their eyes and use touch to identify the different items on their completed collages.

Candy Math

1. Give each child 10 candy-coated chocolate pieces. Use them to count the "sick men."

2. Take one man away at a time until only one is left. Count after each subtraction.

3. When only one "man" is left, ask, "What did this one man say to Jesus? How many men remembered to say thanks to Jesus for healing them?"

Count Your Blessings

Bible reference: Psalm 118:1

PREPARATION

Materials Needed

Large dishpan filled with sand

Small "blessings" to hide under the sand. You might include a toy car, tiny doll, small can of food, small book, toy animals, sock, or seed package. Be sure to include a picture of Jesus.

DEVOTION

Part 1

God is so good to us. He loves us so much. He gives us everything we have. He gives us … *Reach under the sand and pull out an object. Discuss that gift from God.* Isn't God good to us?

Let the children approach one at a time and reach under the sand for one of God's gifts. Discuss each object. God gives us all these gifts—and many more. He knows just what we need. *Hold up the picture of Jesus.* But this is God's best gift of all. He sent Jesus to be our Savior. Jesus loved us so much, He died for our sins. Let's fold our hands right now and thank God for all His wonderful gifts to us.

Dear God, thank You for cars and clothes and people who love us. Thank You for food and books and furry animals. But, most of all, thank You for sending Jesus to be our Savior. Amen.

Part 2

Lead the children in the following motion poem.
Thank You, God, for stars in the sky.
(Wiggle fingers overhead.)
Thank You for birds flying so high.
(Wave arms as if flying.)
Thank You for legs and ears and eyes.
(Point to each body part as it is named.)
And thank You for friends just my size.
(Touch top of head.)
Thank You for shoes that help me run.
(Run in place.)
And thank You for the shining sun.
(Point to the sky.)

NOVEMBER

Blessing Banners

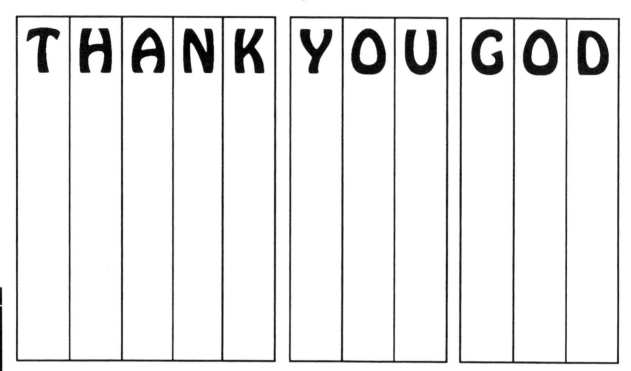

Thank You for buzzing honeybees. *(Move hand as if following the flight of a bee.)* Thank you for always loving me! *(Hug self.)*

Prayer

Thank You for the world so sweet,
Thank You for the food we eat,
Thank You for the birds that sing,
Thank You, God, for everything. Amen.

Songs

The following songs are from *Little Ones Sing Praise*, CPH:

"God Is So Good"

"He Has Done Marvelous Things"

"Thank You, Loving Father"

"The Lord Is Good to Me"

Books to Read

Why I Love You, God, Michelle Medlock Adams, CPH, 2002.

Macaroni and Cheese, Hot Dogs and Peas, Christine Hickson, CPH, 1999.

Whoo! Moo! Cock-a-Doodle Doo!, Christine Harder Tangvald, CPH, 2000.

Ribbit! Roar! Quack, Quack, Quack!, Christine Harder Tangvald, CPH, 2000.

Puzzle

1. Cut a large sheet of poster board into the shape of a cornucopia. Cut the cornucopia into puzzle pieces.

2. Let each child select a puzzle piece and draw on it a picture of something he or she is thankful for.

3. Staple the puzzle back together on the bulletin board, or glue it to a full sized sheet of poster board and display it in the classroom. Use the heading "Thank You, God."

Colorful Cornucopia

1. Make cardboard templates for fruits and vegetables: a circular one that can become either an orange, apple, potato, or tomato; a banana; a bunch of grapes; a curvy squash; large pumpkin; etc.

2. Let the children trace around the cardboard templates onto construction paper of appropriate colors. Then let them cut out their fruits and vegetables and use them to fill the cornucopia thanksgiving puzzle.

3. Discuss the different colors of all the fruits and vegetables God made.

Count Your Blessings

Glue pictures or small objects showing God's blessings on large index cards under the appropriate numeral from 1 through 10. For example: on the first card glue one old key under the numeral 1; on the second card glue two buttons under the numeral 2; on the third card glue pictures of three children under the numeral 3. Let the children use the cards to count the blessings and identify the numerals.

Blessing Banners

1. Write each letter in the phrase "Thank You, God" at the top of long strips of paper. Tape the strips in order along a wall or above the windows. See the illustration on the facing page.

2. Let the children look through magazines and catalogs to find pictures of items for which they are thankful that begin with the letter at the top of each strip.

3. Glue or tape pictures under the appropriate letter. For example: under the letter "T" the children might tape pictures of a telephone, teddy bear, T-shirt, etc. Give help as necessary.

NOVEMBER *

Promises to Keep	Bible references: Psalm 145:13; Acts 13:32; Mark 1:1–8

PREPARATION

Materials Needed

Christmas card showing nativity scene with baby Jesus

Draw a happy face on one paper plate and a sad face on another. Tape a craft-stick handle to the bottom of one of the paper plates. Staple or glue the two plates together so one side shows a happy face and the other side shows a sad face.

DEVOTION

Hold up the sad face. This is Annabel. She is so sad today. Look at her sad face. Why do you think she is sad? *Let children suggest reasons.* Those are all things that might make Annabel sad, but I know the real reason she's sad today. It's because her big sister promised to teach her how to roller skate today. But then her big sister had lots of homework to do, and she couldn't keep her promise to Annabel. Now Annabel is so sad.

Sometimes we feel sad like Annabel. Maybe your mother promised to buy you a treat at the store, but then she ran out of money and couldn't afford your treat. Or maybe your grandpa promised to take you to the park, but then his car broke down and he couldn't go. Or maybe your friend promised to play outside with you, but then he had to go somewhere with his father and couldn't play.

The Bible tells us about a promise God made a long time ago. God loved His people so much that He promised to send them something special. God promised to send them a Savior to save them from their sins. So the people waited and waited and waited. And then one day God kept His promise. Baby Jesus was born! *Show Christmas card nativity scene.* Baby Jesus grew up to be the Savior. He died to save all people from their sins. God kept His promise! God always keeps His promises!

Show happy face. This is Annabel now. She has a happy face because she knows God always keeps His promises. She knows God sent baby Jesus. And now she's going to start getting ready for Jesus' birthday. Let's join her! *Choose one of the enrichment activities and let the children begin to "prepare the way for the Lord" (Mark 1:3).*

Handprint Wreath

Plastic Lid Ornament

Plastic Lid

Construction Paper

Christmas Card

Prayer

Dear God,
Someone's coming, someone special
And I know just who.
Jesus is coming. Jesus is coming.
He's Your promise come true.
Amen.

Songs

"Advent Wreath Song," *Little Ones Sing Praise*, CPH.

"Jesus, Our Good Friend," *Little Ones Sing Praise*, CPH. (Sing stanza 1 only.)

"Light One Candle," *Little Ones Sing Praise*, CPH.

"Someone Special," *All God's People Sing*, CPH.

Books to Read

A Family Christmas: Advent Calendar and Storybook, Yolanda Browne, CPH, 2000.

First Festivals Christmas, CPH, 2001.

My More-than-Coloring Book About Christmas, Cathy Speiler, CPH, 1999.

The Savior God Sent, Kelly A. Rainbolt, CPH, 2000.

Advent Candle

1. Score a 12-inch candle into 24 sections.

2. Each day light the candle and spend a few minutes helping the children "prepare the way for the Lord." Sing carols, pray, make Christmas ornaments, tell Bible stories, etc.

Advent Calendar

1. Cut a large Christmas tree shape from poster board. Let the children paint the tree green.

2. Cut 24 circles from colored construction paper. When the paint is dry, glue the circles onto the poster-board tree to look like ornaments.

3. Post on the wall or bulletin board.

4. Purchase Christmas stickers. Each day affix one sticker inside a circle on the tree.

5. Then count how many circles still need stickers. That's how many days till Christmas. Remind the children to "prepare the way for the Lord."

Handprint Wreath

1. Help each child trace around his or her hand onto green paper. Cut out.

2. Assemble overlapping handprints to form a wreath. Curl some of the "fingers" around a pencil if desired.

3. Place the wreath on the door under these words: "Hands for Jesus."

Plastic Lid Ornaments

1. Give each child a plastic lid from a margarine tub or coffee can.

2. Help the children trace around the lid and cut out a red or green circle.

3. Glue the circle inside the plastic lid.

4. Let each child glue a nativity scene from an old Christmas card onto the red or green circle.

5. Write "God's Promise Kept" on each ornament. If desired, add glitter.

6. Use a punch to make a hole at the top of the lid. Thread yarn through to hang.

Advent Services

Send home an invitation for the families in your class(es) to attend the Advent services your church offers. Encourage them to take part in this midweek worship celebration as a reminder of God's promise kept.

DECEMBER

Wait for the Lord
Bible reference: Psalm 27:14

PREPARATION

Materials Needed

Five small dolls   Kitchen timer (optional)   Advent calendar or regular December calendar

DEVOTION

Hold up first doll. Sammy wanted to go to the playground. "Is it time yet?" he asked his mother. *"Wait* just a minute," she said. So Sammy waited and waited and waited. *Set the timer for one or two minutes.* Let's sit quietly and see how long Sammy waited. *Sit quietly until the timer rings.* Did that seem like a long time? It was only a minute or two, but it seemed so long because we were waiting for something to happen. It's always hard to wait.

Hold up second doll. Yolanda always looked at the pink bicycle at the toy store. "Can I please have that bicycle?" she asked her father. *"Wait* until you are five," said her father.

Hold up third doll. Kimiko thought her grandmother made the best cookies in the world. "I really wish I had some of your cookies to eat," she told her grandmother on the telephone. *"Wait* until I come to visit," her grandmother said.

Hold up fourth doll. Carlos loved to swing high. He knew how to move his body back and forth to go higher and higher. "Can I swing now?" he asked his teacher. *"Wait* for the next turn," his teacher said.

Hold up fifth doll. Casey had a new kite with an extra long tail. The wind today was perfect for kite flying. "Will you help me get my kite up in the air?" he asked his big brother. *"Wait* until I finish my homework," his brother said.

Long ago God promised Adam and Eve He would send a Savior. Adam and Eve waited and waited. Abraham counted the stars in the sky while he waited for Jesus. David sang songs and wrote psalms to help him wait for Jesus. John the Baptist told all the people to get ready for Jesus while he waited. Mary sang and prayed to God while she waited for Jesus.

But then one night in a small stable in a town called Bethlehem, something wonderful happened. Jesus the Savior was born. The waiting was over!

Now we're waiting for Jesus' birthday to come. It's so hard to wait and wait for Christmas. Each day seems to take so long.

DECEMBER

Let's count how many days until Jesus' birthday. *Use an Advent calendar or regular calendar to count the days until Christmas.* Only *(fill in the correct number)* days until Christmas. It's getting closer. Let's spend some time getting ready for Jesus. *Sing carols or try one of the enrichment activities now.*

Prayer

Teacher: Dear Jesus, it's hard to wait.
Children: We love You, Jesus.
Teacher: But we are happy today.
Children: We love You, Jesus.
Teacher: We know Your birthday is almost here.
Children: We love You, Jesus.
Teacher: Thank You for being our Savior.
Children: We love You, Jesus.
All: Amen.

Songs

Choose several favorite Christmas carols to sing with the children. Singing helps the children "prepare the way for the Lord" and makes the waiting more bearable. The following suggestions are from *Little Ones Sing Praise* by CPH:

"Advent Wreath Song"

"Jesus, Our Good Friend"

"Light One Candle"

Sing the following song to the melody "Row, Row, Row Your Boat." Let the children ring bells, clap their hands, dance, and jump as they sing.

Ring, ring, ring the bells. Listen! Do you hear?
Refrain: Jesus Christ is coming soon. Christmas time is here.
Clap, clap, clap your hands. Clap so loud and clear. *Refrain.*
Sing, sing, sing out loud. Let your

voice spread cheer. *Refrain.*
Dance, dance, dance for joy. Dance with someone dear. *Refrain.*
Jump, jump, jump up high. Jump both far and near. *Refrain.*

Books to Read

Advent Is for Waiting, Donna R. Rathert, CPH, 1986.

Away in a Manger, Debbie MacKinnon, CPH, 2000.

My More-than-Coloring Book about Christmas, Cathy Spieler, CPH, 1999.

Where Is Jesus?, CPH, 1999.

Nativity Puzzle

Waiting Game

1. Cover a box with Christmas wrapping paper.

2. Place into the box slips of paper with simple, instant activities to help the children wait for Christmas. Suggestions: sing "Away in a Manger;" put an ornament on the Christmas tree; color a picture for baby Jesus; place a figure in the nativity scene; ring bells; mail a Christmas card; etc.

3. Each day let one child choose an activity from the box and lead the class in carrying out the activity.

Touch and Tell

Place Christmas items (ribbon, candy cane, bell, ornament, cookie cutter, wrapping paper, star cutout, etc.) in a large Christmas stocking. Let the children take turns reaching into the stocking to identify each object by touch alone.

Dough Handprints

Dough handprints make great gifts for children to give to their family members.

1. Mix 1 cup cornstarch, 2 cups salt, and 1¼ cups cold water.

2. Cook over low heat, stirring constantly, until the mixture becomes very thick. Cover and let cool. Keep covered until you are ready to use.

3. Give each child a ball of dough to knead and play with. When they are finished, help them flatten the ball and press a handprint into it.

4. With a drinking straw, make a hole at the top of each handprint to thread a ribbon or piece of yarn through.

5. Lay handprints on a flat surface and let dry at room temperature for a few days.

6. Thread ribbon or yarn through the hole in the top of each handprint.

Painted Wrapping Paper

1. Cover a large table with white tissue paper.

2. Set disposable plates or trays of red and green tempera paint next to plastic Christmas cookie cutters (bells, stars, angels, candy canes).

3. Let the children dip the cutters into the paint and print onto the tissue paper.

4. Use the paper to wrap Christmas gifts for family members.

Nativity Puzzles

1. Cut old Christmas card scenes showing the nativity into simple puzzles of four to six pieces. The illustration on the facing page gives an example.

2. Let the children assemble the puzzles as they wait for Jesus' birthday.

3. Store each puzzle in its own envelope to keep the pieces separate.

Advent Services

Continue to invite your families to midweek Advent services. Post the dates and times in a prominent place for all to see.

DECEMBER *

Happy Birthday, Jesus

Bible reference: Luke 2:1–20

PREPARATION

Materials Needed

Photocopy the Christmas puppets on page 50. Color the puppets, then paste or tape craft sticks to the back of each puppet and press into a play dough base so the puppets can stand alone.

Hay or shredded newspaper "hay"   Juice or milk

Birthday cake with candles   Decorate the room with Christmas decorations

DEVOTION

Today is a special day. Did you see the decorations? Did you see the cake? Today we are going to have a birthday party. Whose birthday is coming soon? That's right, Jesus' birthday is coming. This is a birthday party for Jesus!

Stand Mary and Joseph puppets where all the children can see them. Mary and Joseph traveled all the way from their home in Nazareth to the town of Bethlehem. They had to write their names in the king's big tax book. The king wanted to count all his people. *Move puppets "down the road."* The road was dusty and hilly. Mary and Joseph felt so tired. They traveled a long way.

At last they saw Bethlehem. Mary wanted to rest. So Joseph looked and looked for a place to stay. But the streets were filled with people, and he couldn't find a room anywhere. Finally Joseph found a place to stay for the night. It was a barn filled with donkeys and sheep and cows. Joseph piled soft hay to make beds where he and Mary could sleep. *Rest puppets on beds of "hay."*

That night something wonderful happened! Baby Jesus was born! *Stand baby Jesus-in-manger puppet.* Mary wrapped her baby in long white cloths and laid Him in the manger where the animals ate.

That night some shepherds sat in the fields watching their sheep. *Stand shepherds and sheep puppets away from Mary, Joseph, and Jesus.* Suddenly a bright light filled the sky. An angel stood in the light. *Stand angel puppet.* "Don't be afraid," the angel said. "I have good news. Today Jesus, the Savior, was born in Bethlehem. Go and see Him." Then the whole sky filled with angels. They all sang beautiful songs to God.

Remove angel puppet. After the angels left, the shepherds hurried to find baby Jesus. *Move shepherds and sheep toward Mary, Joseph, and baby Jesus.* And they found Him. They were so happy.

They kneeled down and prayed to baby Jesus.

The shepherds told everyone what had happened. "Jesus, the Savior, is born!" they shouted.

That's what happened the night Jesus was born. It was a happy, happy night. Let's sing "Happy Birthday" to Jesus to show Him how happy we are that He was born. *Continue the party by lighting the candles on the birthday cake and singing "Happy Birthday" to Jesus. Let the children help you serve the cake and juice or milk. After the children finish their cake and drink, lead them in the following motion poem.*

One night in Bethlehem, Mary and Joseph slept on the hay.
(Rest head on hands.)
Cows said moo and the donkeys said neigh.
(Make sounds like the animals.)

Then baby Jesus was born for all.
(Outstretch arms.)
He was a baby so tiny and small.
(Hold hand close to floor to indicate "small.")

Angels sang, "Jesus is born tonight."
(Cup hands around mouth.)
Shepherds hurried to see the great sight.
(Walk quickly in place.)

Mary rocked baby Jesus so new.
(Pretend to rock baby.)
He was born for me and for you.
(Point to self and then others.)

Shape Manger

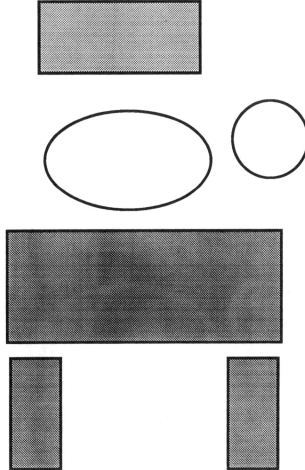

Christmas Puppets

50

Prayer

We're so glad You were born on that first Christmas, Jesus! Thank You for coming to be our Savior. Amen.

Songs

The following songs are from *Little Ones Sing Praise*, CPH:

"Advent Wreath Song"

"Away in a Manger"

"Happy Birthday, Lord"

"In a Little Stable"

"Light One Candle"

Christmas Books to Read

The Jesus Tree, Annetta E. Dellinger, CPH, 1991.

Jesus Is Born!, Claudia Courtney, CPH, 1999.

Jesus Is Born: Connect-n-Play Puzzles, CPH, 2000.

Just Look in the Stable, Christine Harder Tangvald, CPH, 2000.

The Real Night before Christmas, Isabel Anders, CPH, 1999.

That Special Starry Night, Jeff Carnehl, CPH, 2001.

ENRICHMENT ACTIVITIES

Happy Birthday, Jesus, Banner

Include this activity as part of the birthday party for Jesus.

1. Write the words "Happy Birthday, Jesus!" on a long sheet of paper.

2. Let the children trace over the letters with glue and sprinkle with two or three colors of homemade glitter. *Homemade glitter recipe:* Fill a jar about half full of dry grits. Add food coloring. Shake until the food coloring evenly covers the grits.

3. When dry, hang in the room as a Christmas decoration.

Shape Mangers

1. Make cardboard templates for large and small rectangles, squares, circles, and ovals. (See page 49.)

2. Help each child trace the templates and then cut out one large and two smaller rectangles, one square, one circle, and one oval.

3. Let the children assemble and glue the manger, as illustrated, on a whole sheet of construction paper.

4. Discuss the story of Jesus' birth as the children work. Help children identify and name each shape as they assemble their mangers.

5. Write "Baby Jesus … Born for (*child's name)*" above each manger.

Christmas Eve and Christmas Day Services

Invite families in your class(es) to worship on Christmas Eve and Christmas Day. If a family does not have a church home, encourage another family to "host" them in worship.

Shining Stars

Bible reference: Matthew 2:1–12

PREPARATION

Materials Needed

Darken room. Shine several small flashlights around the ceiling as you begin the devotion. Cut paper star as illustrated on page 54. Use gold paper or color white paper gold.

DEVOTION

On a clear night, the sky is filled with bright shining stars. *Shine flashlights on the ceiling.* They seem to twinkle and glow in the sky. Some stars shine yellow; others glow. Some stars look bright and clear; others look fuzzy and dim.

Did you ever wonder where the stars go during the day? They're still in the sky. *Turn on lights. Keep shining flashlights.* But we can't see them because the sunlight fills the sky and keeps us from seeing the light of the stars. We can see stars only when the sky is dark.

When Jesus was born, God had a special star shine right over the place where He lived. Some Wise Men, who lived far away, saw this star in the sky. They traveled a long, long way to find Jesus. Finally they found Him with Mary and Joseph. The Wise Men knelt down and prayed to Him. Then they gave Jesus beautiful presents of gold and perfume and expensive spices.

God wanted the Wise Men to find Jesus. That's why He made the beautiful, bright star shine in the sky. God wants us to find Jesus too. The stars remind us Jesus was born for us. He came to be our Savior. Every time we see the stars shining in the night sky, we can remember Jesus, our Savior.

Begin unfolding paper star. And then we can become shining stars to tell other people about Jesus and His love. When we love Jesus, our hearts are so filled with His love that our lives shine and we become shining stars.

Prayer

When all the stars shine bright at night,
I think about the Wise Men's sight.
A beautiful star shone bright and clear,
Shouting, "baby Jesus is here."

I love that baby in the hay.

Shining Stars

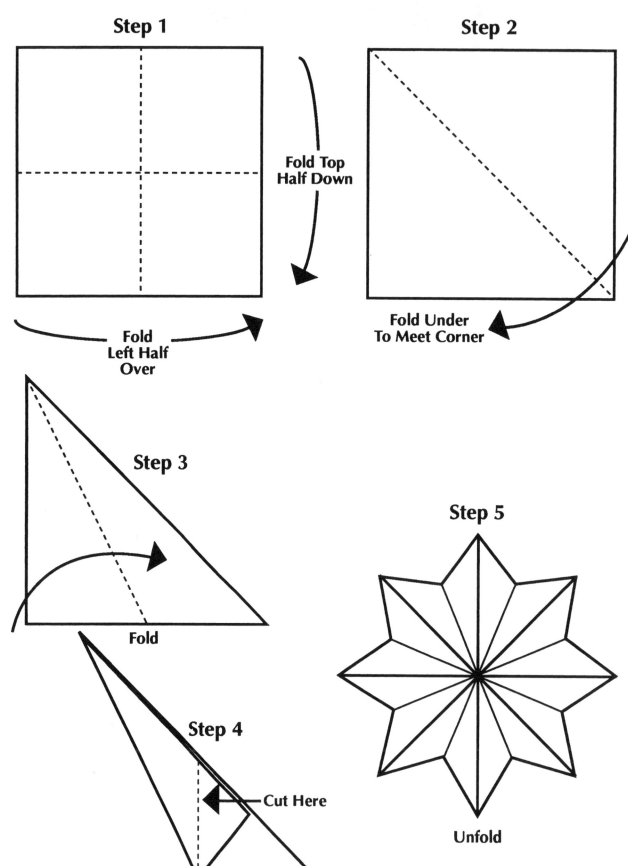

Step 1

Fold Top Half Down

Fold Left Half Over

Step 2

Fold Under To Meet Corner

Step 3

Fold

Step 4

Cut Here

Step 5

Unfold

54

He's with me each and every day.
His love fills my heart to the brim.
And my life shines with love for Him.
Thank You, God, for sending Jesus.
Amen.

Songs

"Jesus, Our Good Friend," stanza 2, *Little Ones Sing Praise*, CPH.

Sing the following lyrics to the melody "Twinkle, Twinkle, Little Star":
Twinkle, twinkle, shining star,
You can shine both near and far.
Shining bright for all to see,
Jesus' love fills you and me.
Twinkle, twinkle, shining star.
You can shine both near and far.

Books to Read

Follow That Star: A Christmas Story, CPH, 2001.

Three Presents for Baby Jesus, Joanne Bader, CPH, 1996.

Toddlers' Action Bible, Robin Currie, CPH, 1998.

The Wise Men: Connect-n-Play Puzzles, CPH, 2000.

ENRICHMENT ACTIVITIES

DECEMBER

Star Size

1. Cut out stars of different sizes.
2. Let the children take turns sorting them in order from largest to smallest.

Star Gifts

1. Help each child assemble a coupon book filled with coupons to give to others. You might like to include coupons saying the following:
   I want to make my bed.
   I want to give you a big hug.
   I want to tell you about Jesus' birthday.
   I want to pick up my toys.
   I want to help you set the table.
2. Let the children decorate their coupons with crayons or markers and gummed stars.
3. Discuss how Jesus' love can shine in us and make us shining stars for Him.

Painting Stars

1. Cut out one star for each child.
2. Let the children use several colors of tempera paint to decorate their stars.
3. Post the stars on the bulletin board described in the following activity.

Shining for Jesus Bulletin Board

1. Place a large picture or cutout of Jesus in the middle of a bulletin board under the words "Shining for Jesus."
2. Surround with cutout and painted stars—one for each child.
3. Place each child's picture in the middle of his or her star.

Apple Stars

1. Cut an apple horizontally to show the star shape made by the core and seeds. (You may also find star fruit in your grocery store.)
2. Discuss with the children the special star that shone the night Jesus was born. Stars remind us of the Wise Men's visit and our best Christmas gift—Jesus.

Growing, Growing . . .

Bible reference: Luke 2:40, 51–52

PREPARATION ← ▬ ▬ ▬ ▬ ▬ ▬ ▬ ▬ ▬ ▬ ▬

Materials Needed

Apple seed

Apple

Apple juice (optional)

Pictures of yourself as a baby, young child, and teenager

DEVOTION

Part 1

Place apple seed inside your closed fist. I have something very small to show you. It's so small I can hide it right here in my closed hand. Would you like to see what I have hidden in my hand? *Show children the apple seed. Let them observe and hold it.* It's a seed. A seed isn't very big. But God makes little seeds just like this one grow and grow into big trees. And do you know what grows on some of those trees? *Hold up apple.* Apples! This juicy, yummy apple grew from a tiny seed just like this one. *If you wish, let all the children enjoy some apple juice.*

God helps things grow. He helps apples and flowers and grass grow. He helps puppies and kittens grow. He helps boys and girls grow too. Every day I see all of you growing taller and stronger and wiser.

When I was a baby, I looked like this. *Show children baby picture of yourself.* Then God helped me grow, and I looked like this. *Show picture of yourself as a young child.* Then God helped me grow a little more, and I looked like this. *Show picture of yourself as a teenager.* And now I look like this. I'm glad God helps us all grow.

Part 2

God helped baby Jesus grow, too.
Baby Jesus grew and grew. Just like you.
Crawled and walked and even talked. Just like you.
Ate and slept and played with toys. Just like you.
Jesus helped His mother work. Just like you.
Jesus helped His father, too. Just like you.
Jesus ran and climbed and jumped. Just like you.
Saw the stars and heard the wind. Just like you.
Jesus talked to God above. Just like you.

Knew that He was always loved. Just like you.

When Jesus was a boy about your age, He probably did lots of the same things you like to do. He played games, said His prayers, washed His face, helped His mother in the kitchen, helped His father build things with wood, shared His toys with friends, and ran and jumped outside. He was just like you in many ways. But in one way, Jesus was not like you at all. Jesus was God's own Son. And Jesus never did even one naughty thing. He died on the cross to save us from our sins. He became our Savior.

Prayer

Thank You, God, for helping me grow taller and wiser and more loving. I love You, God! Amen.

Songs

"Young Jesus Grew in Naz'reth," *Little Christian's Songbook*, CPH.

"Jesus, Our Good Friend," stanzas 3 and 4, *Little Ones Sing Praise*, CPH.

Books to Read

My Book About Life in Jesus' Time, Robert Baden, CPH, 1998.

So Big!, Christine Harder Tangvald, CPH, 2000.

So Smart!, Christine Harder Tangvald, CPH, 2000.

Resource: *Daily Life at the Time of Jesus*, CPH, 2001.

Growing Hands

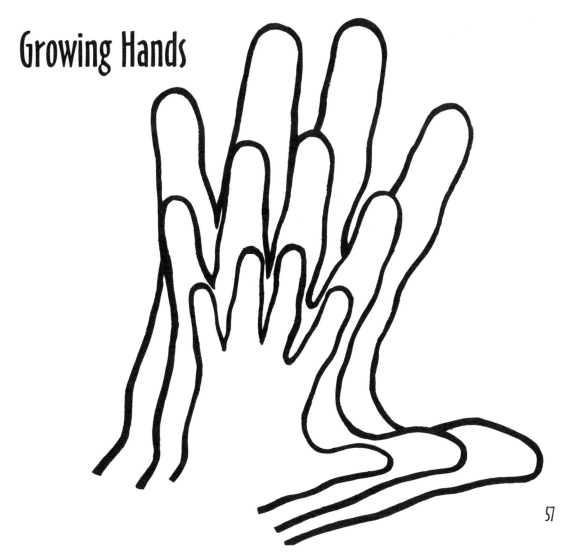

Growing Sequence Pictures

1. Ask each child to bring three photographs showing him or her as a baby, a toddler, and a preschooler.

2. Discuss what the children did at each age and how God is helping them grow.

3. Let each child glue or tape the pictures to a sheet of construction paper in the correct sequence to show growth.

4. Write these words at the top of each paper: "God Helps Me Grow."

Growing Hands

1. Prepare a worksheet showing the outline of an adult's hand with a baby's hand outlined inside it, as suggested by the illustration on the previous page.

2. Help the children place their hands between the other two hand prints and trace around their own hands to see how their growth compares.

Wood-Shop Helpers

Jesus probably helped Joseph in his carpentry shop. Let the children experience working with wood as they make wood sculptures. Pile small pieces of wood on a table and let the children glue them together to make creative sculptures. Also provide pieces of sandpaper so the children can sand the wood.

Kitchen Helpers

Jesus probably helped Mary carry water from the well. Let the children practice pouring and measuring water. Provide plastic pitchers, measuring cups and spoons, tubs, funnels, and lots of towels for spills.

Growing Bread

1. Bake some bread with the children. (If you don't want to bake bread from scratch, purchase frozen loaves of bread dough.)

2. Set out loaves and let the children watch them grow and grow.

3. Explain how God helps bread grow. He gives us yeast to make the bread rise.

4. Discuss how faith in God grows in us through the power of the Holy Spirit.

Fabulous Faces

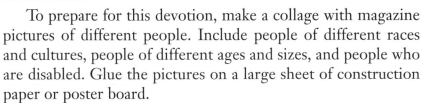

Bible reference: John 13:34

PREPARATION

To prepare for this devotion, make a collage with magazine pictures of different people. Include people of different races and cultures, people of different ages and sizes, and people who are disabled. Glue the pictures on a large sheet of construction paper or poster board.

Materials Needed

Old magazines

Poster board or construction paper

Glue stick

DEVOTION

Part 1

Show children the collage you have made. This is my people collage. It shows lots and lots of people. People come in all sizes and shapes and colors. Everyone in the world is different. No two people are exactly alike. Some people are tall and some are small. Some people are old and some are young. Some people are black and some are white. Some people are boys and some are girls. Some people walk and some people ride in wheelchairs. We are all God's special children.

Point to a person in the collage. Give him or her a name. Tell something about that person. For example: This is Kimiko. She lives far across the ocean in Japan. Kimiko has special slippers she always puts on as soon as she goes into her house. *Then ask,* "Does Jesus love Kimiko?" *Repeat with other pictures as long as children remain interested.*

Does Jesus love all these people? Yes, He certainly does. Jesus loves everyone!

Part 2

Seat the children in a circle. Today we're going to play a game. I'm going to whisper a Good News message to *(name children sitting next to you).* Then we'll pass the Good News message all around the circle. Each of you will whisper the message to the person sitting next to you. *Whisper "Jesus loves you" to the child sitting next to you. Encourage the children to pass the message all the*

JANUARY

way around the circle. Now everyone has heard the Good News message. Let's all shout it together. Jesus loves you!

Part 3

(Optional: for use on Martin Luther King, Jr.'s birthday)

Not so very long ago, a man had a wonderful dream. He knew that Jesus loves everyone—big, small, black, white, young, and old. This man dreamed that all people would live together in love and peace. And he dreamed that all people would work and talk and pray together. Then they could solve their problems instead of fighting with one another. This man was Martin Luther King, Jr. He was the pastor of a church. And he won a special prize for all the work he did.

Prayer

Pray this litany with the children. Ask them to respond after each line with "Thank You, Jesus."

Jesus loves short people.
Jesus loves tall people.
Jesus loves big people.
Jesus loves small people.
Jesus loves boys.
Jesus loves girls.
Jesus loves old people.
Jesus loves babies.
Jesus loves me.
Jesus loves you.
Jesus loves everyone!

Song

"Jesus Loves the Little Children," *Little Ones Sing Praise*, CPH.

Books to Read

These books will help give the children an understanding of various cultures.

My Dream of Martin Luther King, Faith Ringgold, Dragonfly Books, 1998.

Tall Body, Short Body, Everybody's Somebody, Mary Hollingsworth, CPH, 2000.

Ten Friends Together, Susan Titus Osborn and Christine Harder Tangvald, CPH, 2002.

Inner City

Jennifer of the City, Corbin Hillam, CPH, 1990.

Whistle for Willie, Ezra Jack Keats, Penguin. 1964.

France

Madeline, Ludwig Bemelmans, Viking Penguin, 1958.

Ukraine

The Mitten, Jan Brett, G. P. Putnam's, 1989.

Appalachia

When I Was Young in the Mountains, Cynthia Rylant, E. P. Dutton, 1982.

Africa

Why Mosquitoes Buzz in People's Ears: A West African Tale, Verna Aardema, Dial Books Young, 1978.

Vietnam

Angel Child, Dragon Child, Michele Maria Surat, Raintree Publishers, 1983.

Hispanic

En Mi Familia (In My Family), Carmen Lomas Garza, Children's Book Press, 2000.

My Very Own Room (Mia Propio Cuartito), Amanda Irma Perez, Children's Book Press, 2000.

JANUARY

African American

Amazing Grace, Mary Hoffman, Dial Books for Young Readers, 1991.

Boundless Grace, Mary Hoffman, Dial Books for Young Readers, 1995.

ENRICHMENT ACTIVITIES

Fabulous Face Collage

1. Let the children cut out magazine pictures to make collages of many different people.
2. Overlap the collages to form one giant collage.
3. Post it on the bulletin board or wall under the heading "Jesus Loves Everyone!"

Around the World Discovery Corner

Set up a table or a corner of the room where the children can learn about other cultures. You might include the following:

Books from the library showing pictures of children in other countries.

Music from other cultures.

Clothing and items the children can use to dress up like people in other parts of the world (hats, sandals, fans, shawls, etc.).

Cassettes that teach a foreign language.

Food from other countries (fortune cookies, pita bread, tortillas, rice, etc.).

Fabulous Words

Teach the children some words in several other languages. Continue this activity throughout the year and use the new words as often as possible in everyday activities.

God's House

DEVOTION

Jesus couldn't stand still. He was excited today. And His feet just wanted to move. Jesus fastened His sandals around His ankles and jumped up and down. *(Jump up and down with the children.)* He skipped back and forth. *(Skip in place.)* He lifted one foot and then the other. *(Lift one foot, then the other several times.)* He practiced running down the road that led to the big church in Jerusalem. *(Run in place.)*

Finally He heard His mother, Mary, calling Him. "Jesus, it's time to leave now." Jesus hurried out the door. He felt so proud. Now He was 12 years old—old enough to worship God at the big church in Jerusalem.

Jesus walked *(walk in place)* and skipped *(skip in place)* and jumped *(jump up and down)* down the road to Jerusalem. But when He finally saw the big church, He ran and ran as fast as He could. *(Run in place.)*

At last Jesus was inside the big church. He prayed. *(Fold hands.)* He sang. *(Cup hands around mouth.)* He listened to God's Word. *(Touch ears with fingertips.)* Jesus felt so happy.

But soon it was time for Jesus and His family to leave Jerusalem. Many people were on the crowded road to go back home. That night Mary and Joseph couldn't find Jesus. They asked everyone they saw, "Have you seen Jesus? Do you know where He is?" But no one had seen Jesus all day.

Mary and Joseph hurried back to Jerusalem. They looked everywhere for Jesus. But they couldn't find Him!

At last they went back to the big church. And there sat Jesus! He was talking to the teachers. Jesus liked learning about God. And He loved the big church so much that He stayed longer than anyone else.

Then Jesus went home with Mary and Joseph. He felt so happy that He ran *(run in place)* and skipped *(skip in place)* and jumped *(jump up and down)* all the way home. Jesus loved being in God's house. And He couldn't wait to go back again.

Prayer

Dear God, I love my church. I love to sing and pray and say "hooray" when I am there. Thank You, God, for my church—a special place to worship You. Amen.

Song

Try this "piggyback" song from *Little Ones Sing Praise*, CPH, to the melody "Here We Go 'Round the Mulberry Bush."

This is the way we dress for church *(stretch arms above head as if putting on a sweater)*;
Dress for church, dress for church;
This is the way we dress for church,
Every Sunday morning.

Continue with:
Walk to church *(walk happily in place)*;
Climb the steps *(climb imaginary steps)*;
Sit in church *(sit up straight and attentive)*;
Stand and sing *(stand and pretend to hold a hymnal)*;
Pray in church *(bow head and fold hands)*;
Leave the church *(walk happily in place)*.

Books to Read

Colors I See in Church, Julie Stiegemeyer, CPH, 2002.

Jesus and the Family Trip, Sarah Fletcher, CPH, 1998.

Things I See in Church, Julie Stiegemeyer, CPH, 1999.

Following Jesus to Church Bulletin Board

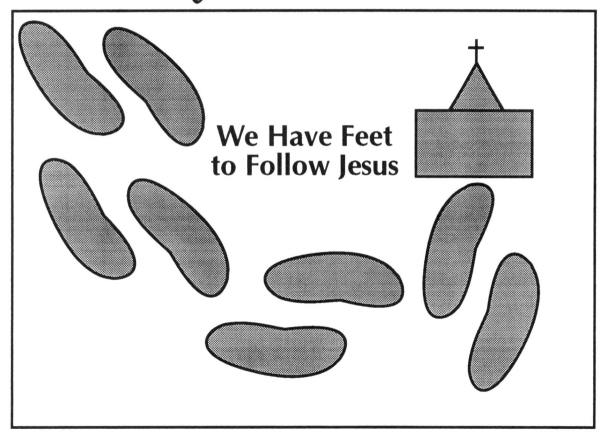

We Have Feet to Follow Jesus

Going to Church Movements

Let the children use their bodies to imitate ways people go to church. They might use transportation:

Drive a car *(pretend to steer the wheel)*

Ride a bicycle *(lie on back and pedal in the air)*

Row a boat *(pretend to row with arms)*

Ride the bus *(bend knees and bounce up and down)*

Ride a horse *(stand with legs apart and pretend to ride)*

Fly an airplane *(extend arms out at sides and move up and down)*

Ride on the train *(rotate arms in front of body and "choo choo")*

Or they might use their own legs:

Walk   Run

Skip   Hop on two feet

Jump on one foot, then the other

Discuss the following with the children: How did Jesus go to church? Did He ride a bicycle? drive a car? fly an airplane? etc.

Visiting God's House

1. Take the children inside the church. Remind them that the church is a special place to worship God.

2. Lead the children around the church and let them use their senses to explore God's house. Let them touch the pews, smell the flowers, listen to the organ, and see the colors in the windows. Take time to count the candles and name all the colors in God house.

3. You might like to sing a song together while visiting the church. "We Are in God's House Today," *Little Ones Sing Praise*, CPH, is especially appropriate.

Muffin Count

1. Set out a 12-cup muffin tin and a container filled with small items such, as buttons, beans, or paper clips.

2. Tape paper circles with the numerals 1 through 12 written on them inside each of the cups of the muffin tin.

3. Let the children take turns placing the correct number of items inside each cup. One button in the cup labeled with "1," and so forth.

4. Review the story as the children work. Remind them that Jesus was 12 years old when He took a trip to the big church.

How Many Feet?

1. Help the children trace around their feet.

2. Cut out the footprints and decorate them.

3. Let them use the "feet" to measure across the table, around the room, up the wall, etc.

4. Keep the footprints to use in the bulletin board idea below.

Following Jesus to Church Bulletin Board

1. Place these words at the top of a bulletin board: "We Have Feet to Follow Jesus."

2. On one side of the board, place an outline of a church with a cross on top.

3. Assemble the footprints for the "How Many Feet?" activity with the footprints going toward the church.

Shoe Match

Bring in various pairs of shoes—baby shoes, work shoes, sandals, tennis shoes, high heels, etc. Mix the shoes up and put them into a box. Let the children pull them out and match the pairs.

Every Part Counts

Bible reference: 1 Corinthians 12:12–31

PREPARATION

Materials Needed

Flannel board body parts assembled to form a complete person

3" x 5" card with each child's name written on it

Tape

DEVOTION

We're going to play a game. *Remove one flannel foot and place it next to a hand on the flannel board.* Let's pretend that one day our foot said, "I'm not as important as this hand. I can't pick things up and carry them like this hand can." That's pretty silly, isn't it? You know what I would tell that foot? I would say, "Foot, you are too just as important as the hand. We need you to take us places. We need you to walk." *Place foot back where it belongs.*

Remove ears and place next to eyes. Now let's pretend that one day our ears said, "We don't want to be ears anymore. We want to be eyes." That would be a problem, wouldn't it? If we had four eyes and no ears, then we couldn't hear any sounds at all. I think we'd better leave our ears where they belong. *Put ears back where they belong.*

God made our bodies so wonderfully. Each part of our body has a special job to do. Our eyes see, our ears hear, our hands touch, and our mouths taste. Each part is just as important as the other parts. When all the parts work together, our body can do many things. It can run and jump and clap and see and hear and touch and taste and bend and wiggle all over.

Our church is like this body. It's made up of many different parts that all work together to do wonderful things. Each of us is a special part of the church. Each of us has a special job to do. *Name each child in your classroom and tell some special way that child excels as a part of the church family. For example you might say: "Kim sings praises to God. Kevin always helps other people. Amanda listens quietly to Bible stories." As you mention each child, tape that child's name card over a part of the body.*

Point to self. I am the church. *Point at the children.* You are the church. We are all important and special parts of God's church. Big or small, short or tall, we all are the church together.

Stained-Glass Windows

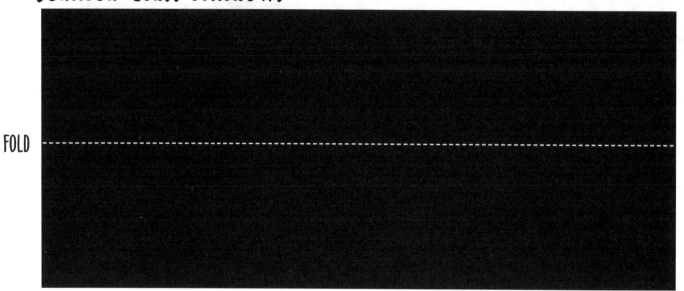

FOLD

Cut Out Designs

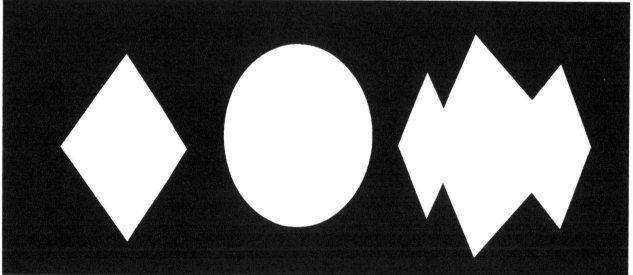

Unfold
Glue Tissue behind Holes

Prayer

Ask the children to join hands and form a circle. Dear God, thank You for Your church. And thank You for each and every person all around the world who follows Jesus. They are all part of Your church. Thank You for *(name each child)*. Amen.

Songs

Sing these songs from *Little Ones Sing Praise* by CPH:

"We Are the Church"

"Our Church Family"

Books to Read

Things I See in Church, Julie Stiegemeyer, CPH, 1999.

Colors I See in Church, Julie Stiegemeyer, CPH, 2002.

ENRICHMENT ACTIVITIES

We Build the Church

Let the children use large blocks to build a church building. If you don't have large blocks available, make some by cutting the tops from clean half-gallon milk cartons and slipping two together to form a solid block.

We Are the Choir

Give each child a bell or rhythm instrument. Let children make their own praise music to accompany songs they have learned. If you wish, you can act as "director" and point to each child when it is time for him or her to play an instrument.

We Make a Banner

1. Cut several shapes of people out of cardboard.

2. Help the children use markers to trace around the shapes onto scraps of fabric and then cut out the shapes.

3. Let the children decorate their people shapes with buttons and yarn. Then let them glue their shapes onto a large piece of felt or fabric.

4. Use a marker to write children's names above their people shapes.

5. Place these words at the top of the banner: "We Are the Church Together."

6. Hang the banner in church or in your classroom.

Stained-Glass Windows

1. Give each child a sheet of black construction paper.

2. Show children how to fold the paper in half lengthwise.

3. Let them cut out designs along the fold.

4. Open the paper and lay it flat.

5. Glue colored tissue paper behind each hole in the paper.

6. Hang the stained-glass window pictures in front of your classroom windows so the sun shines through them.

JANUARY

Helping Hands

Bible reference: Matthew 4:18–22

PREPARATION ← ▬ ▬ ▬ ▬ ▬ ▬ ▬ ▬ ▬ ▬ ▬ ▬

Materials Needed

Six toy people—Jesus, Peter, Andrew, James, John, and an extra one to represent the children.

Place the toy representing Jesus on the table or floor as you begin the devotion below. Add the others as they are mentioned. Move the toys as necessary.

DEVOTION

Jesus had so much work to do.
He preached. He taught. He healed, too.
He thought, *Where could some helpers be?*
They're at the Sea of Galilee!

Jesus started out for a walk.
He saw two men and stopped to talk.
The men were fishing with a net.
The fish swam in; the men got wet.

"Stop," Jesus said. "And come with Me.
Soon fishers of men you will be."
The men dropped their nets right away
And followed Jesus that very day.

Peter, Andrew, and Jesus walked on.
Soon they saw James and his brother, John,
In a boat with nets up to their knees.
"Come," called Jesus. "My helpers you'll be."

James and John followed Jesus, too.
Now Jesus says to each of you,
"I love you, Kim and Greg and Dee,
Be My helper and follow Me."

Jesus calls each of us to follow Him and be His helper. How can we help Jesus? *Let the children suggest ways we can be a helper for Jesus. Reinforce the idea that any time we help another person, we also help Jesus. When we show love to someone, we show love for Jesus. Then sing this song to the melody "Mary Had a Little Lamb."*

I can help do Jesus' work,
Jesus' work, Jesus' work.
I can help do Jesus' work,
And this is what I'll do.

I'll tell a friend about His love,
About His love, about His love.
I'll tell a friend about His love,
His helper I will be.

I'll wash the dishes squeaky clean,
Squeaky clean, squeaky clean.
I'll wash the dishes squeaky clean,
His helper I will be.

Continue with the following stanzas:
I'll plant some pretty flower seeds
I'll share my toys with a friend
I'll make my bed and smooth the sheets
I'll pick up all my toys at night
I'll tell someone that "I love you"
I'll make my grandma smile and laugh
I'll make a card for someone sick

Prayer

Dear Jesus, I want to be Your helper too, just like Peter, Andrew, James, and John. I want to use my hands and arms and feet and legs and mouth to help You. I want to show everyone how much I love You. Be with me, Jesus. Amen.

Songs

"Jesus Wants Me for a Helper," *Little Ones Sing Praise*, CPH.

"I Am Jesus' Helper," *The Little Christian's Songbook*, CPH.

Books to Read

In His Footsteps, Cathy Drinkwater Better, CPH, 2000.

Bible Discovery Devotions, Martha Larchar, CPH, 2000.

Going Fishing

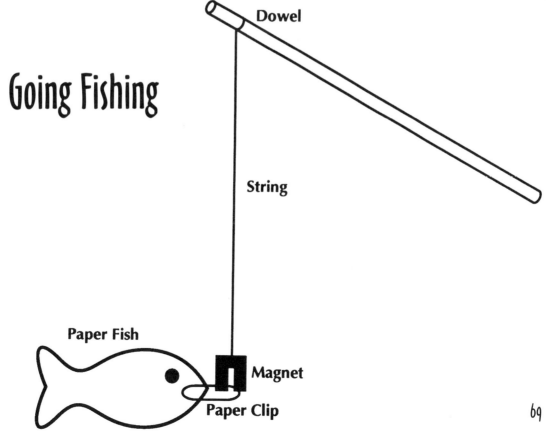

Dowel

String

Paper Fish

Magnet

Paper Clip

Helping Hands

1. Mix a batch of finger paint using the recipe that follows, and let the children experiment with it. You might want to let them finger paint on old cookie sheets. Talk about all the things our hands can do.

2. After the children have created a finger-paint design they are pleased with, press a sheet of white paper on top of their design, then lift the paper quickly. This will reproduce the children's painting on the paper and preserve their designs.

3. Before they wash their hands, let the children press their handprints onto a paper tablecloth. Use the tablecloth at snack time to remind them of their "helping hands."

Finger Paint Recipe

> 2 c. flour
> 2 t. salt
> 3 c. cold water
> 2 c. hot water
> Food coloring

Gradually add cold water to flour and salt. Beat until smooth. Add hot water and cook over low heat until glossy, stirring constantly. Add food coloring as desired. Store in refrigerator.

Going Fishing

1. Cut out fish shapes from construction paper.

2. Attach a paper clip to each fish.

3. Attach a piece of string to the end of a dowel to make a fishing pole.

4. Tie a magnet at the end of the string.

5. Overlap several pieces of blue construction paper on the floor to make a "fishing pond."

6. Let the children take turns catching fish by touching the magnet to the paper clips.

Kitchen Helpers

Let the children help prepare their own snack. Pour whipping cream into a jar. Add a pinch of salt if desired. Take turns shaking the jar until the butter (curds) separates from the whey. Pour off the whey. Let the children use table knives to spread the butter on crackers.

Singing Helpers for Jesus

Make a cassette tape of the children singing some of their favorite songs about Jesus. Include rhythm instruments if desired. Give the tape to your church office to share with shut-ins and hospital patients when the pastor or human care committee visits them.

Bubbling Love

Bible reference: 1 Corinthians 13

PREPARATION

Materials Needed

Bottle of bubbles with wand inside

Make a large construction-paper heart and draw a cross in the center. Fold heart and place it inside an envelope.

Song "Love in a Box" (on page 128).

DEVOTION

Today I brought something to school that I think you all like to play with. *Hold up bottle of bubbles.* Do you know what is inside this bottle? That's right. Liquid to make bubbles. Lots and lots of bubbles. Bubbles that float. Bubbles that shimmer. Bubbles that pop. *Take out wand and blow some bubbles.*

Keep blowing bubbles until after you sing the song. Bubbles are fun. Everybody wants to reach out and grab a bubble. But we can't. Bubbles just float and pop, and float and pop. They keep coming and coming. They make us happy, and they make us laugh.

Jesus' love is like these bubbles. It makes us very, very happy. And we can't stop it. It just keeps coming and coming. We can't keep Jesus' love closed up in a bottle. His love will always come bubbling out.

Sing or recite stanza three of "Love in a Box." Then stop blowing bubbles.

I brought something else this morning. I wonder what it is. Shall I open it? Do you want to see what's inside?

Open envelope and take out heart with cross. It's a big valentine heart with a cross right in the middle of it. Let's see if we can figure out what this means. Hearts mean love, don't they? When we see a heart, we think of love. And crosses mean Jesus, don't they? Every time we see a cross, we think of Jesus dying on a cross for our sins. So a heart with a cross in it must mean that Jesus is sending us His love. And Jesus loves us so-o-o much. Because of Jesus and His love, we can be God's children and live with Him forever. That's the best valentine of all!

When Jesus' love fills our hearts, something wonderful happens to us. *Begin blowing bubbles again.* Our lives bubble over with His love, and we share His love with everyone we know.

Sing or recite stanza five of "Love in a Box."

FEBRUARY

Prayer

Dear Jesus, fill our lives with love—
The love that comes from You above.
And help us show that love to all—
Young and old and big and small. Amen.

Songs

These songs about joy in Jesus are from *Little Ones Sing Praise* by CPH:

"Happy All the Time"

"I Have the Joy"

"Love in a Box"

"Love, Love, Love"

Books to Read

Celebrate Feelings, Heidi Bratton, CPH, 2000.

My B-I-B-L-E, Cathy Drinkwater Better, CPH, 1999.

Why I Love You, God, Michelle Medlock Adams, CPH, 2002.

Fold

Valentine Pillows

72

Valentine Pillows

1. Follow the pattern on the facing page and cut out hearts.

2. Cut crosses from the center of each heart as illustrated.

3. Cut two hearts from white paper for each child, or let the children trace and cut out their own hearts and crosses.

4. Have the children paint the hearts with red and pink paint.

5. When the hearts have dried, staple two-thirds of the way around the outside of the hearts.

6. Lightly stuff tissue paper between the hearts and finish stapling.

Tissue-Paper Hearts

1. Make a cardboard template of half a heart.

2. Show the children how to make their own hearts by placing the template along the fold of a sheet of paper, tracing around it, and cutting along the line.

3. After cutting out their hearts, let the children use red, pink, and white tissue-paper squares and liquid starch to make a collage on the cutout hearts. Use paintbrushes to brush the starch over the tissue paper to make it stick to the paper. Encourage children to overlap their tissue-paper squares to create a layered look.

Valentine Bingo

1. Divide paper or large index cards into nine squares.

2. Fill in each square with numbers one through nine, making sure to mix up the numbers so cards are as different as possible.

3. Let the children play bingo by placing candy valentine hearts over their squares as each number is called.

4. After nine calls, everyone's a winner!

Gelatin Hearts

1. Mix three envelopes of unflavored gelatin and two small packages of flavored red gelatin with two cups boiling water.

2. Stir until the gelatin dissolves.

3. Pour into a 13" × 9" pan and chill until firm.

4. Use a heart-shaped cookie cutter to cut gelatin into heart shapes.

5. Lift hearts from the pan and serve as a special Valentine treat.

Bubbling Bubbles

1. Pour warm water into a plastic dishpan.

2. Add liquid dish detergent.

3. Let the children dip and squeeze sponges into the dishpan to make bubbles.

FEBRUARY*

Follow the Leader

PREPARATION

You will need to gather several props in advance for this two-part devotion.

Materials Needed

Part 1

Simple outline of a cloud

Bible

Picture of a sheep

Paper crown

Part 2

Quarter and $1 bill

Penny and $5 bill

DEVOTION

Part 1

I love to play follow the leader. When I was just about your age, my friends and I played follow the leader all the time. We jumped and skipped and walked like ducks—whatever the leader did, we did too. And then after a while, someone else took a turn being the leader. It was fun to be the leader, and it was also fun to be a follower.

God gives us good leaders. He gives us leaders who help us do His work. God's special book, the Bible, tells about many leaders that He chose.

God chose Moses to lead His people on a long, long walk all the way from a land called Egypt back to their home. Moses didn't really want to be the leader. He told God he didn't know how to be a leader. But God said, "Don't worry, Moses, I will help you." And He did.

Hold up drawing of cloud. God put a big, special cloud in the sky to help Moses lead the way home. At night the cloud glowed like fire so God's people would always know He was with them.

God also chose Joshua to lead His people. *Hold up Bible.* Joshua studied God's Word so he would know what God wanted him to do.

David was a boy who watched sheep in the fields. *Hold up picture of sheep.* But God chose Him to be a king. *Hold up paper crown.*

Another person God chose to be a leader was Josiah. Josiah

was just eight years old when he became king. *Place paper crown on head of one of the children.* That's not much older than you. But he was a good king, and he did God's work.

Hezekiah was another leader God chose. Hezekiah knew it was important to pray and ask God for help. *Fold hands.* He often talked to God in prayer.

God chose Paul to lead people by telling them about Jesus. Paul used his mouth to talk about Jesus *(touch lips)* and his fingers to write many letters telling about Jesus *(pretend to write).*

God has chosen many good leaders. And God has also chosen you to help do His work. God has special work for each of you to do.

Sing "God Chose Me," Little Ones Sing Praise, *CPH, to the melody "Twinkle, Twinkle, Little Star."*

God chose me, and God chose you.
We have special work to do!
Helping people every day,
We can sing, and we can pray.
God chose me, and God chose you.
We have special work to do.

Part 2

This month we remember the birthdays of two other people God chose as leaders. These people aren't written about in God's book, the Bible, like Moses and David and Paul. But they were important leaders who led our country.

George Washington was the first president of the United States of America. Sometimes we call him the "Father of our Country." He led people many years ago when our country was just beginning, first as a general in the army and then as president. We see his picture every time we look at a quarter or $1 bill. *Show children the pictures of George Washington on the quarter and $1 bill.*

Then pass them around the room.

Abraham Lincoln was another president of our country who has a birthday this month. He lived in a log cabin when he was a boy. But Abraham Lincoln read books and studied very hard. When he grew up, he was elected president. He led our country when many people were fighting, and he worked to make sure that all people were free. We see his picture every time we look at a penny or a $5 bill. *Show children the pictures of Abraham Lincoln on the penny and $5 bill. Then pass them around the room.*

Prayer

Dear God, thank You for giving us good leaders. Help us to lead others to You. Amen.

Songs

"This Little Gospel Light of Mine," *Little Ones Sing Praise*, CPH.

Books to Read

Crossing the Red Sea, Patricia A. Hoffman, CPH, 1999.

The Adventures of Moses, Andy Robb, CPH, 2000.

Tumbling Walls of Jericho, Patricia A. Hoffman, CPH, 1999.

Where Is Moses?, CPH, 1999.

Follow the Leader

Let the children take turns demonstrating a movement (touching toes, running in place, bending knees, swinging arms, clapping hands, etc.) for the others to follow. You might sing this song to the melody "Are You Sleeping?" to introduce each child:

Now it's your turn. Now it's your turn.

Come on up. Come on up.

You can be the leader. You can be the leader.

Go this way and that. Go this way and that.

Leader of the Band

Let the children take turns leading the others in a marching band. Give the leader a rhythm stick to use as a baton.

Pennies and Quarters

Place a container of pennies and quarters on the table. Let the children sort the pennies into one pile and the quarters into another.

Give each child 10 pennies. Put them in a line, count them, subtract them, add them, stack them.

Red, White, and Blue

Let the children tear sheets of red, white, and blue construction paper into pieces and overlap them to make a torn-paper collage on pennant-shaped paper. If you wish, let them glue a penny and/or quarter onto the collage.

FEBRUARY

A Special Book

PREPARATION

Materials Needed

Two finger puppets—one for Mary, one for Martha. Follow the pattern on page 78. The puppets can be cut from paper and taped or cut from sturdy cloth and sewn together. Draw hair and facial features onto the paper or cloth. Or you may wish to glue yarn hair and tiny button eyes onto the puppets.

A Bible

DEVOTION

Knock. Knock. Knock. *Make knocking sound, then hold up Martha puppet.* Martha opened the door. There was Jesus! He had come to visit. How exciting!

Martha wanted everything to be nice for Jesus' visit. *Make Martha puppet hurry around busily.* So she started to cook a fine meal. She baked fresh bread. She dusted all the furniture.

Martha was afraid she wouldn't have time to finish all her work. She wished her sister, Mary, would help her. *Hold up Mary puppet.* But Mary just sat and listened to Jesus. *Sit Mary puppet on your knee.*

At last Martha said, "Jesus, please tell Mary to help me. I have so much work to do."

Jesus smiled at her. "Mary is doing the most important thing of all. She's learning about God. Why don't you sit down and listen too?"

Hold up both puppets. Mary and Martha both loved Jesus. They both wanted to make Him happy. Martha had so many things to do. But Jesus said that Mary was doing the most important thing of all. What was that most important thing? That's right. Jesus told Martha that learning about God was the most important thing of all. *Put puppets away.*

Hold up Bible. God has given us a special book to help us learn about Him. This book is the Bible. The Bible is God's very own book. It tells us many wonderful and true stories. But the most important thing the Bible tells us is that God loves us. He loves us so much, He sent Jesus to save us from our sins.

Lead children in the following motion poem.

The Bible is God's special book,

FEBRUARY

(Cup hands to form open book.)
And He has told us where to look,
(Point to open "page" on one hand.)
To find out all we need to know
(Make sweeping circle with arms.)
About the love He has to show.
(Cross arms on chest.)
When I listen and really hear,
(Point to ears.)
I know that God is always near.
(Bring both palms toward shoulders.)
And when I look and really see,
(Point to eyes.)
I know that God loves you and me.
(Point to others and then self.)

Prayer

Dear God, thank You for giving us the Bible. We love to listen to the wonderful stories it tells. Help us to learn more and more about Your love. Amen.

Songs

Sing these songs from *Little Ones Sing Praise* by CPH:

"The B-I-B-L-E"

"Jesus Loves Me, This I Know"

Books to Read

Bible Discovery Devotions, Martha Larchar, CPH, 2000.

A Child's Garden of Bible Stories: Classic Edition, Arthur W. Gross, CPH, 2001.

Mary and Martha's Dinner Guest, Swanee Ballman, CPH, 1998.

My B-I-B-L-E, Cathy Drinkwater Better, CPH, 1999.

Sit Down, by Mary Manz Simon, CPH, 1991.

Finger Puppets Pattern

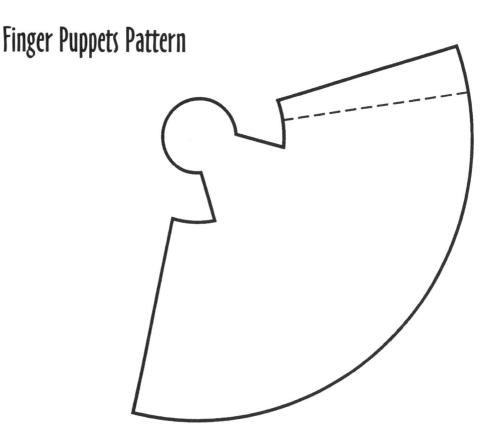

It's a Puzzle

1. Gather pictures illustrating various Bible stories. Possible sources include old Sunday school leaflets, religious magazines, and greeting cards.

2. Glue the pictures onto poster board.

3. Cut the pictures into five or six pieces.

4. Place the Bible story puzzles into separate envelopes and let the children take turns putting them together. Then review the Bible stories.

My Own Bible

1. Help the children make a simple "Bible." Cut hearts from white paper.

2. Let the children decorate the hearts with paint, crayons, or markers.

3. After the paint has dried, let the children glue a craft-stick cross to the middle of each heart.

4. Glue the heart and cross onto a piece of white paper.

5. Write "Jesus Loves Me" at the top of the paper.

6. Use two pieces of black construction paper to make a cover for the "Bible."

7. Staple the three pieces of paper together to form a book.

8. Use white chalk to write "*(Name)'s* Bible" on the cover.

Bibles Everywhere

Display as many Bibles as possible. Include cloth Bibles, leather Bibles, children's picture Bibles, large Bibles, tiny New Testaments, Bible storybooks, Bibles in other languages, etc.

Let the children look at them, hold them, and "read" them. Stress that these are all God's book, the Bible, although they look different.

String Bible Stories

1. Seat the children in a circle. While holding a ball of yarn in your hands, begin to tell a Bible story. Choose a story the children know well.

2. Stop telling the story and pass the ball of yarn to the child sitting next to you. Continue to hold the end of the yarn in your hands.

3. Let the child holding the yarn ball continue telling the Bible story. Give help as necessary.

4. Then that child stops telling the story and passes the yarn ball to the next child in the circle.

5. Continue until all the children have had a turn and the yarn ball is back in your hands.

FEBRUARY*

Happy Again

Bible references: Ephesians 4:32;
Colossians 3:13

PREPARATION ◄ — — — — — — — — — — —

Materials Needed

Two puppets

Piece of paper with crayon drawings

DEVOTION

Miranda: *(holds up a piece of paper filled with crayon drawings)* Look, Theodore! Look at my b-e-a-u-t-i-f-u-l picture. I worked and worked to make it look just right.

Theodore: *(looks at Miranda's picture)* Well, you should have worked longer. Your picture is yucky. It's just a bunch of scribbles.

Miranda: It is not just scribbles!

Theodore: Oh, yes it is!

Miranda: It's not.

Theodore: It is.

Miranda: It's *not!* And you're the meanest boy I ever saw. *(Miranda hits Theodore)*

Theodore: *(crying loudly)* She hit me! She hit me!

Teacher: Wait a minute, you two. Fighting isn't Jesus' way to solve our problems.

Miranda: But Theodore said my picture was scribbling!

Theodore: And Miranda hit me!

Teacher: I can see that you're both angry and hurt. Theodore, you shouldn't have called Miranda's picture scribbling. You hurt her feelings. Everyone has a special way of creating art. And Miranda, you shouldn't have hit Theodore. Hitting hurts too. Do you two want to stay angry and hurt?

Miranda: No. I feel miserable.

Theodore: I guess not.

Teacher: I know how you both can feel happy again. Would you like that? *(Puppets nod heads yes.)* Jesus' way to solve our problems has a long name. It's called forgiveness. Jesus' way is special because it not only solves our problems, it makes us happy again, too.

Miranda: It's hard to forgive Theodore.

Theodore: And my arm still hurts where she hit me.

Teacher: Sometimes it is hard to forgive. But we could ask God to help us forgive one another.

Miranda: Okay. I'll ask Him. Dear God, please help me forgive Theodore. And help him forgive me too. Help us to be happy friends again. Amen.

Teacher: Do you feel better now?

Miranda: I guess so. I'm not so angry any more.

Theodore: Miranda, I'm sorry I called your picture scribbling.

Miranda: And I'm sorry I hit you. I hope your arm feels better.

Theodore: It hardly hurts at all any more. And my heart feels better too. I'm happy again.

Miranda: Me too! Jesus' way is the best! Forgiveness really does make us happy again.

(Miranda and Theodore hug each other.)

Theodore: Let's go play with my car collection.

Miranda: Okay, Theodore. And then maybe my mom will give us chocolate chip cookies. *(Puppets walk off together.)*

Prayer

Help the children say their own simple prayers to ask God to help them forgive after arguments and fights.

Songs

The song "I'm Sorry," found in *Little Ones Sing Praise* (CPH), offers another way to help children learn to forgive one another. This song can be sung any time misbehavior occurs.

Huggie Bears

Happy Again Pictures

Let the children use yellow and white paint on dark blue paper to make "happy again" pictures. Stress that Jesus' way of forgiveness restores our happiness and takes away our sad feelings.

Huggie Bears

1. Make photocopies of the huggie bear shown on the previous page.

2. Let the children decorate one or more huggie bears with markers, crayons, stickers, etc.

3. Place the huggie bears in a basket or box somewhere in the classroom.

4. Encourage the children to give huggie bears to one another when forgiveness is needed.

Happy Again Cookies

> 3 c. oatmeal
>
> 1½ c. brown sugar
>
> 1½ c. flour
>
> 1½ c. butter or margarine
>
> 1½ c. t. baking powder

Put all the ingredients in a large mixing bowl. Let the children work in pairs to knead it, mix it, smash it, and squish it with their (washed) hands. The more you mix, the better it tastes. Then let the children roll the dough into small balls and place the balls on a cookie sheet. Bake for 10–12 minutes at 350 degrees.

Exercise for Two

Have the children exercise in pairs.

- Choo-choo. Have two children lie on their backs with the bottoms of their feet touching and raised off the floor. Keeping their feet together, the children should bend and straighten their legs and pedal against each other.

- Rowboat. Have two children sit on the floor placing the bottoms of their feet together and holding hands. They should take turns leaning backward and forward as they "row."

- Balloon toss. Have two children work together to keep a balloon from touching the ground.

Hot Line to Heaven

Bible references: 1 Thessalonians 5:16–18; James 5:13; Psalm 91:15

PREPARATION

Materials Needed

Toy or real telephone

DEVOTION

Last night I wanted to talk to my friend. My friend doesn't live near me. She lives far away. But I really wanted to talk to her and tell her some exciting news. How do you think I managed to talk to my friend even though she lives far away? That's right. *Hold up telephone.* I used the telephone. I dialed her number on my telephone and talked to her just like she was right here with me.

The telephone is a wonderful invention. We can talk to people far away or to people right next door. We can quickly call the fire department to come and put out a fire, or we can talk and talk for a long time to our grandma and grandpa. We can call a store to find out what time they open, or we can call our friends to see if they can come over to play. *If you wish, let the children role-play dialing the telephone and talking to someone.*

When we want to talk to God, we don't need a telephone. We have our own hot line to heaven. It's called prayer. All we have to do is talk to Him just like we talk to one another. We can talk to God about anything. If we are happy, we can laugh with God. If we are sad, we can tell Him all about it. If we are afraid, God will listen and be with us. If we see a beautiful flower, we can thank Him for making it.

Sometimes when we call someone on the telephone *(dial the phone and listen for an answer)*, the phone just rings and rings. No one answers our call. The person we are calling isn't home. That makes us sad because we can't talk to them. Sometimes the person we are calling is on the phone to someone else and the line is busy.

But one of the best things about prayer is that we can always talk to God. He's always there to hear our prayers. He's always listening, and He's always at home. He's never busy talking to someone else. Day or night, at home or in the car, outside or inside, God hears and answers our prayers.

MARCH

Prayer

Dear God, I know You're always there,
Each time I come to You in prayer.
Help me Your loving child to be.
And thank You, God, for loving me!
Amen.

Songs

Sing these songs from *Little Ones Sing Praise* by CPH:

"God, Our Father, Hear Your Children"

"Jesus Listens When I Pray"

"We Pray for Each Other"

Books to Read

Daytime Prayers, Yolanda Browne, CPH, 2000.

Grandma, What Is Prayer?, Katherine Bohlmann, CPH, 2002.

The Lord's Prayer, CPH, 2000.

Sleepytime Prayers, Yolanda Browne, CPH, 2000.

Tuck Me In, God, Christine Harder Tangvald, CPH, 1998.

Thank-You Prayer Bag

Motion Poem

Let the children follow your motions in this activity that shows some of the many postures of prayer:

I fold my hands and bow my head.
(Fold hands and bow head while sitting.)
Sometimes I kneel beside my bed.
(Kneel on floor with folded hands.)
I stand and raise my arms above.
(Stand with arms and head raised up.)
Holding hands makes a circle of love.
(Join hands in a circle.)
Lots and lots of ways to say,
"I love You, God," each time I pray.
(Hug self.)

Thank-You Prayer Bag

1. Fill a plastic or paper bag with items the children might thank God for giving them. Include such items as a leaf, family picture, bandage, small stuffed animals, can of food, crayon, picture of a house, egg carton, rock, toy car, sock, etc.

2. Let each child reach into the bag and choose an item.

3. Begin a thank-You prayer to God. Pause and let the children continue the prayer by naming the items they are holding. Close the prayer by holding up a cross (you can use two craft sticks glued together) and thank God for sending Jesus to be our Savior.

Prayer Collages

1. Give each child a paper plate.

2. Let the children glue items onto the plate to remind them of things they might like to pray to God about. Items may include bandages, canned food labels, family pictures, cross or picture of Jesus, leaves, pictures of animals and insects, pictures of homes and clothing, etc.3. Write these words on the plate: "God Hears Us Pray."

4. Punch a hole at the top of the plate and thread a piece of yarn through the hole.

5. Let the children hang the collages in the classroom as prayer starters. Or encourage them to take the collages home to serve as prayer starters with their families.

A Litany of Adoration, Confession, Thanksgiving, Intercession, and Petition

Adoration

Teacher: God, You are so good and loving to us.
Children: Hear our prayer.

Confession

Teacher: Forgive us for the times we forget to be good and loving to the people around us.
Children: Hear our prayer.

Thanksgiving

Teacher: Thank You for puppies and Popsicles and panda bears.
Children: Hear our prayer.

Intercession

Teacher: Be with our friends who are sad or sick.
Children: Hear our prayer.

Petition

Teacher: And help us have a happy, happy day.
Children: Hear our prayer.

MARCH ✳

Hosanna! Hosanna!

Bible reference: Matthew 21:1–11

PREPARATION ⬅ — — — — — — — — — — — —

Materials Needed

Toy horse and male rider

Several fabric scraps

Some leaves

DEVOTION

Begin the devotion with the following clapping poem. Clap once for each number and count aloud as you clap. Have the children clap in rhythm with you.

1

1, 2

1

1, 2

1, 2, 3

Clapping is a happy way.

1

1, 2

1

1, 2

1, 2, 3

To say "praise, praise, and hooray!"

1

1, 2

1

1, 2

1, 2, 3

Listen, listen, as I say,

1

1, 2

1

1, 2

1, 2, 3

Jesus is with us today!

Jesus loves us so much, and He is so good to us. That makes us want to praise Him all the time, doesn't it? Clapping is one way we can praise Jesus. Singing is another way. Dancing, playing instruments, and painting pictures for Jesus are even more ways we can praise Him.

One day, lots and lots of people had a happy praise celebration for Jesus. On that day, Jesus was close to the town of Jerusalem. He told two of His helpers, "Go find a donkey in the town. Untie it and bring it to Me." The helpers led the donkey back to Jesus. *Walk toy horse across table.* Jesus climbed onto the donkey's back and rode into Jerusalem. *Place rider onto toy horse.*

Jerusalem was full of people. They had come for a big festival. When the people heard that Jesus was coming, they hurried to meet Him. Boys and girls stopped their games and ran to see Jesus. Men and women stopped their work and joined the children. Sick people and old people and tall people and short people—many, many people went to meet Jesus.

Some people put their coats on the road. *Place scraps of fabric on table.* Others cut palm branches and laid them on the road. *Place leaves on table with fabric scraps.* They made a carpet of coats and palm branches for Jesus to ride on.

"He's coming! He's coming!" a little boy shouted. *Walk horse and rider toward fabric scraps and leaves.* The people crowded around Jesus and the donkey. Some walked beside Him. Some followed behind. *Continue walking horse and rider over fabric scraps and leaves.* And everyone shouted, "Hosanna! Hosanna! Praise God! Hosanna!" Boys and girls and men and women waved their palm branches and shouted praises to Jesus all the way through Jerusalem. "Hosanna! Hosanna! Praise to Jesus!"

Prayer

Thank You, Jesus, for loving us so much. Your love makes us want to shout "Hosanna! Hosanna! We love You too." Amen.

Songs

Lead the children in praising God with these songs from *Little Ones Sing Praise* (CPH):

"Hallelujah, Praise Ye the Lord"

"Hosanna! Hosanna!"

Books to Read

Hurry, Hurry, Mary Manz Simon, CPH, 1990.

Jesus Enters Jerusalem, Jane Fryar, CPH, 1993.

The Modest King, Claudia Courtney, CPH, 1999.

The Story of Easter: Giant Flap Book, CPH, 1999.

The Week that Led to Easter, Joanne Larrison, CPH, 2001.

MARCH

Palm Sunday Parade

1. Let the children dramatize Jesus riding into Jerusalem. First, let them cut palm branches from green construction paper. Add some plastic flowers and pieces of cloth as additional props.

2. Help the children form two lines facing each other.

3. Lead them in singing "Hosanna! Hosanna!" Wave paper palm branches and plastic flowers and lay pieces of cloth on the ground as "Jesus" walks through.

Praise Pretzels

Pretzels are a traditional Lenten food. They are usually shaped in the form of two arms crossed in prayer as a reminder of prayer and repentance. Let the children help you make pretzels. After kneading the dough, give each child a piece of the dough to shape into a praise pretzel as he or she wishes.

1 pkg. dry yeast	4 c. flour
1½ c. warm water	2 T. sugar
1 egg	1 t. salt

Combine yeast and warm water. Add egg to flour, sugar, and salt. Add flour mixture to yeast and water mixture. Knead until smooth and elastic. Pinch off pieces. Shape as desired. Place on greased cookie sheet. Brush liberally with water and salt. Bake at 425 degrees F. for 10–15 minutes. Makes about 24 pretzels.

Hosanna Action Poem

As you share this action poem with the children, let them run and jump and hop in place as indicated.

"Hosanna! Hosanna!"
Hear all the children sing.
They run. They jump. They hop
To see Jesus, the King.
"Hosanna! Hosanna!"
With palms and coats so new.
They run. They jump. They hop.
They try to see Him too.
"Hosanna! Hosanna!"
The children stretch so tall.
They run. They jump. They hop.
Here comes the King of all!

MARCH

Why Good Friday Is Good

Bible references: Matthew 27:32–66; Mark 15:16–47; Luke 23:33–56; John 19:17–42

PREPARATION

Materials Needed

1. Assemble these items in a small bag or box:
   small cross, nails, coins, black paper or cloth, sponge, white cloth, stone, numeral 3.
2. Use blocks or paper to make a large cross on the floor. As you begin this devotion, ask the children to sit on the floor around the large cross.
3. Show the children each item as it is mentioned in the Bible story. Then place that item somewhere on the large cross.

DEVOTION

One sad day, Jesus walked slowly down the road. Soldiers were taking Him to a hill outside the city. Jesus carried a big wooden cross on His back. *Hold up cross.* The cross was very heavy. And Jesus felt so tired and sad.

The soldiers saw a man named Simon coming down the road. "Carry the cross for Jesus," they said. So Simon lifted the heavy cross from Jesus and carried it on his own back.

At the top of the hill, the soldiers nailed Jesus on the big wooden cross. *Hold up nails.* Jesus hurt so much. The soldiers made fun of Him. People in the crowds said bad things about Jesus and yelled at Him. But Jesus didn't yell back. Instead, He prayed for them. "Father, forgive them," He prayed.

Two robbers who stole money were on crosses next to Jesus. *Hold up coins.* One robber yelled bad things about Jesus. But the other robber began to believe Jesus was the Savior. "Lord, remember me," he called from his cross.

"Today you will be in heaven with Me," Jesus called back.

It was daytime. The sun shone brightly in the sky. But suddenly everything was dark as night. Hold up black paper or cloth. The darkness lasted three hours.

Jesus had been on the cross for a long time. "I am thirsty," He said. Someone dipped a sponge into vinegar and gave it to Jesus. *Hold up sponge.* A little later Jesus cried out, "It is finished." And He died. His work on earth was done.

The day Jesus died is called Good Friday. Good Friday makes us feel sad because Jesus hurt so much and died. We might not think Good Friday is "good" at all. But Good Friday brings us some very Good News. Jesus suffered and died to save us from all our sins. Now people have forgiveness.

MARCH

89

Later that first Good Friday, some friends of Jesus took His body down from the cross. They wrapped His body in a clean white cloth and laid it in a grave. *Hold up white cloth.* Then they rolled a big stone in front of the door to the grave. *Hold up stone.* They went home feeling sad.

Jesus' friends felt sad because they didn't remember the best news of all. Three days later Jesus came alive again! *Hold up numeral 3.* He's alive now, and He will never die again. He'll always be with us. He'll always help us. And He'll always love us. Now that's good news!

Prayer

Dear Jesus, thank You for suffering and dying on the cross for us. Thank You for loving us so much. We love You too. Amen.

Songs

Sing these songs from *Little Ones Sing Praise* by CPH:

"Do You Know Who Died for Me"

"Glory Be to Jesus"

"I Love to Tell the Story"

Books to Read

The Easter Cave, Carol Wedeven, CPH, 2001.

Easter ABCs, Isabel Anders, CPH, 1999.

God's Love at Easter, Joy Morgan Davis, CPH, 2002.

My More-than-Coloring Book About Easter, Cathy Spieler, CPH, 1999.

The Week that Led to Easter, Joanne Larrison, CPH, 2001.

Lenten/Easter Mobile Patterns

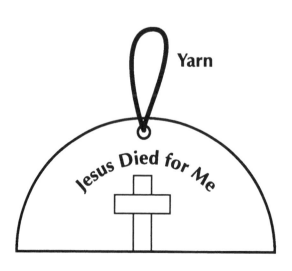

Yarn

Making Crosses

1. Let the children use sugar cubes to make crosses. Stick the cubes together with glue or frosting.

2. Use large blocks to make crosses on the floor.

3. Cut crosses from poster board or old file folders. Use double-sided tape to fasten the crosses in the middle of a sheet of white paper. Let the children paint over the crosses and onto the paper with tempera paint. After the paint has dried, lift the crosses off the paper. A cross outline will remain. Use the cardboard crosses on a bulletin board display or let the children decorate them with paper or plastic flowers for Easter.

Empty Cross and Growing Grass

1. Let each child glue two craft sticks together to form a cross.

2. Fill empty margarine tubs or milk cartons (cut off top half) with potting soil, one for each child.

3. Stand the wooden cross in the soil.

4. Sprinkle grass seed over the potting soil, press down, and water.

5. Place in a sunny window and watch the grass grow around the cross.

6. Remind the children that the empty cross tells us Jesus died for our sins, and the growing grass tells us He is alive again.

Lenten/Easter Mobile

1. Help the children assemble mobiles as shown on page 90. Provide each child with half of a paper plate or a half-circle cut from white, heavy stock paper.

2. On one side of the mobile make a masking tape cross under the words "Jesus Died for Me."

3. Let the children color grass and sky and glue on cotton-puff clouds.

4. On the other side draw a simple Easter lily outline under the words "Jesus Rose for Me."

5. Let the children fill the flower outline by gluing on tiny pieces of torn or cut paper to form a mosaic pattern.

6. Thread yarn through a hole at the top and hang.

MARCH

*

91

Alleluia!

Bible reference: John 20:11–18

PREPARATION

Materials Needed

Two balls of play dough. Shape the balls of play dough as you tell the story. The first ball will be formed into Jesus' tomb. The second ball will be formed to represent Mary and Jesus.

Empty plastic eggs. Hide enough plastic eggs around the classroom so each child will find one.

DEVOTION

As you begin to tell the Easter story, pick up the first ball of play dough. Pull off a lump of the dough. Shape the lump into a stone. Shape the remaining play dough into an open cave. Place the play dough stone next to the play dough cave.

On the first Easter long ago, very early in the morning, Mary came to a cave. Jesus was buried inside.

Pick up the second ball of dough. Divide it into two pieces. Roll into logs to represent figures. Place the Jesus figure off to the side. Move the Mary figure toward the cave.

When Mary got to the cave, she looked inside. She could hardly believe what she saw! Jesus' body was gone! There were two angels sitting where Jesus' body had been. Mary felt so sad. Tears ran down her face. One of the angels asked, "Why are you crying?"

Mary answered, "Jesus is gone! I don't know where He is." *Move Jesus figure behind Mary figure.* Mary turned and saw a man standing behind her. "Who are you looking for?" the man asked.

Mary thought the man was the gardener. "I'm looking for Jesus," she sobbed.

The man said, "Mary!"

Then she knew who the man really was. "Jesus," she cried. "Jesus, You are here!" *Move Mary figure back and forth with excitement.*

"Go and tell all My friends that I am alive," said Jesus.

So Mary hurried to tell Jesus' friends the wonderful news. *Mary figure hurries away.* "He is alive!" she shouted. "Jesus is really alive!"

What a happy, happy day that first Easter must have been for Mary and the rest of Jesus' friends. Easter is a happy, happy day for us, too. Easter tells us the happiest news of all: Jesus is alive!

Hold up one of the plastic eggs. At Easter time, we see lots of

Easter eggs. That's because Easter eggs tell us the Good News about Jesus. This morning when I arrived at school, I hid Easter eggs just like this one around our room. If you look carefully, I'm sure you all will find one. *Let children get up one by one to hunt for an egg. Give help or suggestions if necessary.*

Did you open your eggs? What did you find inside? That's right. Nothing was inside the eggs. That's why these eggs tell us the happy news of Easter. When we look inside them, they're empty. When Mary looked inside the cave that first Easter morning, did she find Jesus? The cave was empty! He was alive!

Look again inside your eggs. Are they empty? That's the happy news of Easter. Jesus is alive! You may take your eggs home to tell others the happy news about Easter. Let's all say the happy news together: Jesus is alive!

Prayer

What a happy day!
I just want to say,
"Jesus is alive!
Hooray! Hooray!"
Amen.

Songs

"Christ the Lord Is Risen Today," *The Little Christian's Songbook*, CPH.

The following songs are found in *Little Ones Sing Praise*, by CPH.

"Hallelujah! Praise Ye the Lord!"

"Jesus Came from Heaven"

"Jesus Loves the Little Children"

"Let Us Sing for Joy!"

"This is the Feast"

Books to Read

Early Easter Morning, Marti Beuschlein and Patricia A. Hoffman, CPH, 1998.

Easter ABCs, Isabel Anders, CPH, 1999.

Easter Cave, Carol Wedeven, CPH, 2001.

God's Love at Easter, Joy Morgan Davis, CPH, 2002.

Jesus Is Alive, Elizabeth Freidrich, CPH, 1987.

My More-than-Coloring Book About Easter, Cathy Spieler, CPH, 1999.

The Story of Easter, CPH, 1999.

The Story of the Empty Tomb, Bryan Davis, CPH, 1998.

Where Is Jesus? Mary Manz Simon, CPH, 1991.

APRIL

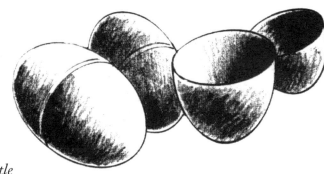

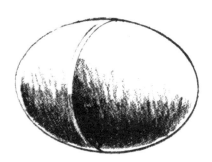

APRIL

Motion Poem

He's risen today.
(Extend arms over head.)
That's why I can say,
(Cup hands around mouth.)
Alleluia! Alleluia! Alleluia!
(Clap hands.)
My Jesus loves me.
(Place hands over heart.)
By my side He'll be.
(Hug self.)
Alleluia! Alleluia! Alleluia!
(Clap hands.)

Egg Sort

Provide empty pie tins or other containers and let the children sort empty plastic eggs by color.

Egg Weigh

Fill plastic eggs with items of different weights. Use pebbles, coins, buttons, etc. Let the children take turns arranging the eggs from lightest to heaviest.

Eggshell Crosses

1. Cut crosses from construction paper.

2. Write "Jesus Is Alive!" on each cross.

3. Let the children decorate the crosses by brushing them with diluted glue and sprinkling crushed colored or white eggshells over the glue.

Marbled Eggs

1. Cut egg shapes from paper.

2. Let each child place a shape into the bottom of a cardboard box.

3. Put marbles into containers of pastel tempera paint.

4. Scoop the marbles out of the paint with spoons and drop them onto the egg-shaped paper in the cardboard box.

5. Tip the box back and forth to roll the marbles around and "paint" the eggs.

Egg Match Game

1. Decorate six or more plastic eggs with adhesive vinyl or paper, rickrack, markers, sequins, glitter, stickers, etc., to resemble decorated Easter eggs. Decorate each whole egg differently.

2. Avoid gluing decorations on the seams of the eggs.

3. Separate the eggs and let the children take turns matching the halves.

Surprise! Surprise!

Bible reference: Matthew 28:6

PREPARATION

The planting activity described below is optional. If you choose to do it, onion bulbs are inexpensive and grow rapidly. You also might like to plant rye grass seed in the paper cups. It will come up in just a few days.

Materials Needed

Several dried bulbs

Potted Easter lily or tulip plant

Pictures of flowers, trees, baby animals, and butterflies

Paper cups, onion bulbs or grass seed, potting soil, spoons (optional)

DEVOTION

Do you like surprises? Can you tell about something happening that really surprised you a lot?

I brought something today that surprised me a lot. Here it is. *Hold up a dried bulb.* This dried-up, brown, ugly bulb is one the biggest surprises I can think of. *Pass the bulb around so the children can look at it carefully.* Last fall I saw a bulb like this at a store. The directions told me to dig a hole, put the bulb into the hole, cover it with dirt, and water it. So I did. Then I waited and waited and waited. And one day, right where I planted that bulb, a plant was growing! I was so surprised! *Show children the potted tulip or Easter lily.* It was hard to believe that such an ugly, dried-up bulb could become a beautiful flower like this one. Do you know what that flower made me think of? It reminded me that Jesus isn't dead anymore. He is alive!

Spring is full of surprises. Everywhere you look something new is happening. *Hold up each picture as you talk about it.* Flowers are growing, new buds and leaves are showing up on all the trees, baby animals are born, butterflies fly out of their cocoons—new life is everywhere! All these happy surprises remind us of the happiest surprise of all—Jesus is alive!

If you wish, give each child a paper cup with the phrase "Jesus is alive!" written on it. Let the children spoon soil into their cups, put in a bulb or grass seeds, and cover it with more soil. Help them water the bulb or seeds lightly.

Prayer

Dear Jesus,
My eyes see bright butterflies.
(Point to eyes.)
My ears hear lambs b-a-a-a.
(Point to ears.)
My hands touch green grass.
(Reach down to touch ground.)
My nose smells new flowers.
(Touch nose.)
My tongue tastes soft rain.
(Touch tongue.)
Thank You, Jesus, for making the world come alive.
(Fold hands.)
They all tell me that You're alive, too!
(Clap hands.)
Amen.

Songs

Sing these songs from *Little Ones Sing Praise*, by CPH:

"I Have the Joy"

"Jesus Came from Heaven"

"Jesus Loves the Little Children"

"Let Us Sing for Joy"

Or try the following "piggyback" song (also from *Little Ones Sing Praise*) to the melody "Are You Sleeping?"

It's a new day, it's a new day
Given by God, given by God.
Join the celebration, join the celebration!
Sing His praise! Sing His praise!

Books to Read

Easter ABCs, Isabel Anders, CPH, 1999.

God's Love at Easter, Joy Morgan Davis, CPH, 2002.

My More-than-Coloring Book About Easter, Cathy Spieler, CPH, 1999.

My Very Blessed Easter Activity Book, Anita Reith Stohs, CPH, 1998.

APRIL

From Caterpillar to Butterfly Bulletin Board

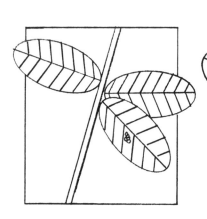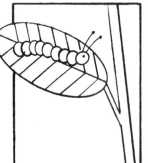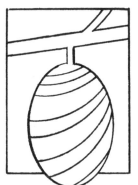

From Caterpillar to Butterfly Bulletin Board

1. Draw outline pictures showing the four stages a caterpillar goes through to become a butterfly: egg on a leaf, caterpillar, cocoon, butterfly. See the illustrations on the previous page to guide you.

2. Let children glue white dots onto the leaves, give the caterpillar pipe-cleaner legs, paste cotton balls onto the cocoon, and make butterflies (see Butterfly Blots below).

Butterfly Blots

1. For each child, crease and fold construction paper in half and cut butterfly shapes.

2. Let each child unfold the paper and dribble several colors of tempera paint onto one half of the butterfly.

3. Fold paper in half along the crease and rub carefully.

4. Open and let dry.

5. Write "Jesus Is Alive!" on each butterfly.

Mother and Baby Animals Match

1. Cut pictures of mother animals and their babies from magazines.

2. Paste the mother's picture on one half of a sheet of paper and her baby's picture on the other.

3. Cut into puzzle piece shapes, using a different design for each.

4. Let the children match the mothers and babies.

Musical Flowers

1. Play soft, slow music. Say to the children, "Curl on up the floor like dried-up bulbs that have just been planted in the ground."

2. As the music plays, say, "Now the rain falls. You're starting to grow."

3. Let the children start to unfold and grow as they move with the music. Say: "Slowly. Slowly. Slowly. Now the sun shines. You're growing a little more. Slowly. Slowly. Slowly. Now more rain. And more sun. You're growing and growing and growing."

4. When the children are standing up straight, say, "You're a beautiful flower—tall and straight."

Musical Butterflies

Again play music, this time faster than in the previous activity. Let the children first pretend to be crawling caterpillars, then curled inside a cocoon, and last flying butterflies.

Soaking Seeds

1. Line a clear glass jar with wet paper towels.

2. Place lima bean seeds between the glass and towels. Press firmly so the seeds are in contact with the damp towels.

3. Put a little water in the bottom of the jar.

4. Add water periodically to ensure that the towels stay moist.

5. Watch the dried seeds sprout to life.

Egg-Carton Flowers

1. Cut paper egg cartons into individual cups.

2. Let the children paint and decorate them.

3. When dry, push and twist pipe cleaners through the tops to form stems.

4. Press play dough into a flowerpot and let the children "plant" their flowers.

APRIL

Noah's Rainy Days

PREPARATION

Tell the story using chalk. Use a wall, free-standing, or lap chalkboard to draw the story as you tell it. Don't hesitate to use only stick figures and geometric lines. The children's imaginations will fill in the details.

Materials Needed

White or yellow chalk for most of the story

Colored chalk for the rainbow

Box of animal crackers

DEVOTION

God told Noah to build an ark. An ark was a big, big, big boat with a roof on it. *Begin drawing an ark.* So Noah did what God told him to do. His ark was very long and very wide and very high. It had lots and lots of rooms. Noah's ark was big enough to hold his whole family and every kind of animal and bird and insect in the world and food for all the people and animals to eat.

Noah and his family climbed into the ark. *Draw Noah and his family walking up a ramp into the ark.* All the animals came too. Lions, lizards, spiders, and sheep all climbed into the ark. *Draw some animals following Noah's family into the ark. Give each child one animal cracker to eat.*

Then God shut the door. *Erase Noah, his family, the animals, and the ramp.* It rained. *Draw raindrops coming down.* And rained. And rained. And rained some more. It rained every day and every night for 40 days and 40 nights. *Draw water under Noah's ark.* But Noah's ark floated safely on top of the water.

At last it stopped raining. *Erase raindrops.* The winds blew and the sun shone. *Draw sun.* The water went away. The ground was dry. *Erase water under the ark.* Noah, his family, and the animals stepped out of the ark. *Draw Noah, his family, and some animals outside the ark. Give each child another animal cracker to eat.*

Noah felt so happy. God had kept them all safe. Then Noah looked up at the sky. He saw a beautiful rainbow. *Use colored chalk to draw rainbow.* It shined red, orange, yellow, green, blue, and purple. God told Noah, "That rainbow is My promise to you. Each time you see a rainbow, remember how much I love you."

Prayer

Dear God, I know You always love me. You love me on rainy days and sunny days. You love me when the wind blows and when it stays calm. You love me on all kinds of days and in all kinds of ways. Thank You, God. I love You too. Amen.

Songs

Sing these songs from *Little Ones Sing Praise* by CPH:

"The Butterfly Song"

"Rise and Shine"

Books to Read

Bible Friends: Who's Hiding? Sally Lloyd-Jones, CPH, 2001.

Drip, Drop, Mary Manz Simon, CPH, 1990.

Hooray! It's a Duck Day, Jennifer Moze Brown, CPH, 1998.

Noah and the Animals: Bible Soft Pockets, Allia Zobel-Nolan, CPH, 2000.

Toddler's Action Bible, Robin Currie, CPH, 1998.

Noah's 2 by 2 Adventure, Carol Wedener, CPH, 1997.

Look at Me . . . I Can Be . . .

Let the children move like different animals. You might introduce the activity with the following poem:

The rain came pouring down

And the water rose high.

Noah and the animals

Stayed warm and always dry.

While living on the ark

The animals liked to play.

Today we can join them

In lots of different ways!

We can stretch like a cat, jump like a kangaroo, hop like a rabbit, waddle like a duck, fly like a bird, slide like a seal, stretch like a giraffe, skip like a lamb, trot like a pony, walk like an elephant, roar like a lion, slither like a snake.

Rainy-Day Pictures

Let the children draw pictures. Then let them use toothpicks to drip white glue onto the picture. The glue will dry clear and leave "raindrops" on the picture.

Animal Shapes

1. Cut out circles, squares, rectangles, and triangles from colorful paper.

2. Let the children experiment by putting the shapes together to make animals.

3. Glue the animal shapes onto a piece of construction paper.

Rainmaking

Hold a pie tin filled with ice cubes over a steaming teakettle. When the hot steam hits the cold pan, the vapor will form drops that fall like rain. **Note:** Be sure to have adult supervision when using electrical appliances or hot water.

Painting with Water

1. Give each child a large brush and a container of water.

2. Let children go outside and use the water to "paint" sidewalks, toys, trees, fences, anything!

3. As the children's "paintings" disappear, ask, "Where did the water go?"

4. Discuss evaporation.

Float and Sink

1. Fill a plastic dishpan with water.

2. Place different items in a bowl next to the pan. You might include a cork, pencil, wooden block, twig, Styrofoam, large nail, bottle cap, quarter, etc.

3. Let the children take turns seeing which items float and which sink.

Noah's Ark Mural

1. Collect a variety of materials to help the children assemble a mural showing Noah's story.

2. Cut a large ark from brown construction paper. Glue onto a long strip of white paper.

3. Let the children add cotton clouds, aluminum foil water, glue raindrops, animals cut from nature and wildlife magazines, Noah and his family cutouts wearing wallpaper or fabric clothes, and a tissue paper rainbow.

4. Hang the completed mural on the wall.

A Rainbow Is a Promise

Bible reference: Genesis 9:13

PREPARATION

Materials Needed

Two puppets

DEVOTION

(Hold up both puppets. A storm is raging outside. One puppet, Theodore, is afraid. The other puppet, Miranda, is not at all concerned about the storm.)

Teacher: Crash! Roar! Cr-r-runch!

Theodore: *(looks around anxiously)* Yikes! I hate storms.

Miranda: Why do you hate storms?

Theodore: All that noise and flashing lightning are too much for me.

Teacher: Boom! Crash! Boom!

Theodore: That's it! I'm going under my bed where it's safe. *(He covers his eyes with his hands and starts to leave.)*

Miranda: Wait a minute, Theodore! I still don't understand why you're scared. The lightning and thunder are like a big fireworks show. They're God's fireworks. Look! See how pretty it is!

Theodore: *(slowly uncovers one eye)* I guess it is kind of pretty, Miranda. But why does it have to make so much noise?

Miranda: God lets us both see and hear His fireworks. They're just two of His special gifts to us. The rain that's pouring down is another of His gifts.

Theodore: Some gift! The rain just means we can't go out to play today.

Miranda: But, Theodore, the rain makes the flowers grow and it gives us water to drink and it …

Theodore: Okay, I understand. I guess the rain isn't so bad after all—especially now that it's ending.

Miranda: *(pointing at something)* Look, Theodore! There's the best and prettiest gift of all. It's a rainbow!

Theodore: Wow! That is pretty. It's red and orange and yellow and green and blue and purple.

Miranda: You know what I like best about rainbows?

Theodore: What's that, Miranda?

101

Miranda: I like the promise God made.

Theodore: What promise?

Teacher: I know the promise Miranda is talking about. *(Both puppets face teacher.)* God promised Noah He would never again send a flood that would cover the whole world. And now each time we see a rainbow, we remember how much God loves us.

Miranda: That's right.

Theodore: Wow!

Teacher: God loves us so much. He loves us and loves us and just keeps on loving us.

Miranda: That's right.

Theodore: Wow!

Teacher: Wow is right! Let's all sing a song to thank God for His promise and for His love.

Lead the children in a song of praise. You might wish to use "Praise Him, Praise Him," Little Ones Sing Praise, *CPH. Be sure the children are familiar with the song you choose. This should be a praise celebration, not a time to teach a new song.*

Prayer

Thank You, God! Thank You for thunder and lightning and rain and rainbows—especially rainbows. Because rainbows remind us how much You love us. We love You too! Amen.

Songs

The following books can be found in *Little Ones Sing Praise*, from CPH.

"Earth and All Stars"

"Praise Him, Praise Him"

"Praise and Thanks"

Books to Read

Bible Friends: Who's Hiding? Sally Lloyd-Jones, CPH, 2001.

Drip, Drop, Mary Manz Simon, CPH, 1990.

Hooray! It's a Duck Day, Jennifer Moze Brown, CPH, 1998.

Noah and the Animals: Bible Soft Pockets, Allia Zobel-Nolan, CPH, 2000.

Peanut Butter Promises, Robin Currie, CPH, 1999.

Toddler's Action Bible, Robin Currie, CPH, 1998.

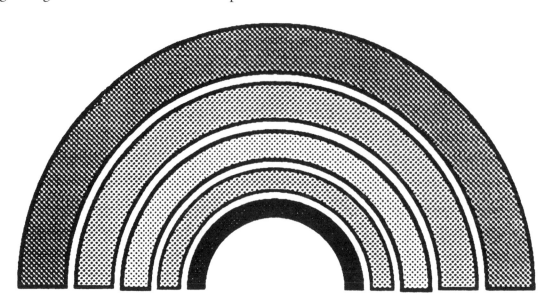

Rainbow Viewers

1. Cut the center from several paper plates. Cover the opening with colored cellophane. Try to have at least red, blue, and yellow.

2. Let the children hold the rainbow viewers up and view the world in different colors.

3. Show them how to combine two viewers to make new colors. For example, red and yellow make orange.

Rainbow of Color Match Game

1. Make a large rainbow from construction paper and place it on a table.

2. Cut small squares of construction paper using the same colors.

3. Let the children match the squares to the colors on the rainbow. You also might like to let the children match jellybeans to the colors on the rainbow.

Color Motion Poem

Give each child construction paper squares of each color from the match game. As each color is named in the motion poem below, the children will hold up that color. Be sure to say the first two lines slowly so the children have time to find the right color.

There's red and orange and yellow too.

Green and blue and purple for you.

A rainbow tells us loud and clear (*cup hands around mouth*),

God loves us, and He's always near (*hug self*).

Rainbows Everywhere

Hang one or more prisms in a window so the sun will shine through them. When rainbows appear, twirl the prism so the rainbows dance around the room.

Rainbow Snack

Make rainbow gelatin by layering three or more colors of gelatin. Allow each layer to set before adding the next. Or bring some rainbow sherbet for a special treat.

Chalk Rainbows

Let the children brush heavy paper with liquid starch and then make rainbows with colored chalk. The liquid starch will intensify the colors and keep the chalk from rubbing off when dry. Encourage the children to use the side of the chalk to make sweeps of the rainbow.

APRIL ✳

103

Where Is Jesus?

Bible references:
Acts 1:1–11; Matthew 28:20

PREPARATION ← ▪ ▪ ▪ ▪ ▪ ▪ ▪ ▪ ▪ ▪ ▪ ▪

Materials Needed

One puppet

DEVOTION

(Hold up puppet with head hanging down sadly.)

Teacher: Good morning, Miranda. How are you today?

Miranda: Not very good. I'm so sad.

Teacher: What's wrong?

Miranda: I can't find Jesus.

Teacher: *(puzzled)* What do you mean?

Miranda: Well, I know Jesus came from heaven to be our Friend and Savior. I know He grew up and helped many people. I know He died on the cross for our sins. I know He came alive again on Easter. *And* I know He went back to heaven. Up, up, up He went until His friends couldn't see Him anymore.

Teacher: That's right, Miranda.

Miranda: That's why I'm sad. Jesus went to heaven. I can't see Him. And I don't know where He is.

Teacher: Now I understand. You're sad because you think Jesus is gone.

Miranda: *(Nods head yes.)*

Teacher: You can stop being sad right now, Miranda. Jesus is here! He's right here with us. We can't see Him, but He's here. Jesus promised, "I will be with you always."

Miranda: *(happier)* You mean Jesus is here in our classroom?

Teacher: He surely is. Jesus is always with us wherever we are.

Miranda: But last week Momma and Poppa and Baby and I went on a trip far away. If Jesus is here, could Jesus find us there?

Teacher: Of course He could. Jesus promised, "I am with you always." That means Jesus is with us on a trip or at home. He's there while we sleep or ride a bike. He's with us when we read a book or eat a peanut butter and jelly sandwich. He is always, always with us!

Miranda: Wow! That's great!

Teacher: It sure is!

Ask the children to follow Miranda and you around the classroom and outdoors if possible. As you walk, lead the children in chanting, "Where is Jesus? Where is Jesus?" Stop at various locations and open your Bible to Matthew 28:20. Read Jesus' promise to the children: "I am with you always."

When you stop at the last location, end this devotion by singing the following "piggyback" song from Little Ones Sing Praise *to the melody "Are You Sleeping?"*

Where is Jesus? Where is Jesus?
Everywhere, everywhere.
What is Jesus doing? What is Jesus doing?
Taking care, taking care.

Prayer

I know You are with me wherever I go.
Thank You, Jesus, for loving me so.
Amen.

Songs

Sing these songs from *Little Ones Sing Praise* by CPH:

"God Is Near"

"I'm with You"

"Jesus Is My Special Friend"

"Jesus Loves the Little Children"

Invisible Pictures

When I'm . . .

Let the children pantomime some activities they might do every day. Introduce each activity with these words, "Where is Jesus when I'm … ?" Add activities such as sleeping, throwing a ball, eating my cereal, riding my bike, sitting in a car, jumping up and down, washing my face, brushing my teeth, putting on my socks, etc.

After each activity the children pantomime, say these words: "Jesus said, 'I am with you always.'"

Moon Balls

Mix a batch of these moon balls with the children.

> 1 c. nonfat dry milk
>
> ½ c. honey
>
> ½ c. peanut butter
>
> ½ c. granola or toasted wheat germ

Mix dry milk, honey, and peanut butter together. Form into balls and roll in granola or wheat germ to coat.

As the children are eating this snack, say,

"We just made moon balls. Where is the moon? Do you think Jesus would be with us if we were on the moon? That's right. He's with us if we are here at school or on a rocket ship flying to the moon. Jesus is with us everywhere and always!"

Invisible Pictures

1. Let the children draw a picture of themselves on white paper. Then let them brush over their self-portrait with invisible paint (cooking oil). When held up to the light, the invisible paint can be seen.

2. Remind the children Jesus is with them all the time. He's like the invisible paint. We can't see Him, but we know He's there with us just like the invisible paint that covers our picture.

3. Hang the pictures in the window where the invisible paint can be seen.

MAY

You Are a Gift

PREPARATION ← — — — — — — — — — —

Materials Needed

Gift-wrapped box

One stick-on bow for each child (placed inside the gift-wrapped box)

Baby doll wrapped in a blanket

Small child's coat (optional)

DEVOTION

Show children the gift-wrapped box. I brought a present to school today. Do you like presents? What was the best present you ever received? *Let children share their memories.*

God gives us so many good presents. He gives us puppies and bicycles and dolls to play with. He gives us homes and food and clothes to wear. He gives us wonderful gifts like mommies and daddies and grandparents to love us.

The Bible tells us about a woman who wanted God to give her a very special present. Her name was Hannah. One day Hannah sat alone in her room and cried and cried. *Wipe eyes with hands.* Hannah had a house to live in, food to eat, clothes to wear, and a husband who loved her. But Hannah still felt so sad. She wanted a baby to love.

Hannah prayed and prayed to God. *Fold hands.* "Dear God," she prayed. "Please give me a baby. I will take such good care of a baby. And I promise to tell my baby about You every day."

God heard Hannah's prayer. Soon she had a beautiful baby boy. *Hold baby doll in your arms.* She named her baby Samuel.

Now Hannah was happy. She loved to rock her baby and play with him. Soon her Samuel could crawl. Then he learned to stand. And Hannah felt so excited when Samuel started to walk and talk. She taught Samuel songs about God. How Hannah loved to sing with her son.

One day Hannah dressed Samuel in a special coat. *Hold up child's coat.* And she took him to church. "God gave me my son," she said. "Now I want my son to love God his whole life."

And do you know what? Samuel did. Samuel loved God his whole life. And each day Hannah thanked God for His wonderful gift of a child.

MAY

Hold up gift-wrapped box again. Would you like to see what is inside this box? *Open box.* Look! This box is filled with bows! There is one bow for each of you because each of you is God's special gift to your family. God gave you to your family. You are God's gift to them. *Place bows on children's hands to remind them they are God's gift.*

Prayer

Thank You, God, for sending me.
As a gift to my family.
Help me show them lots of love.
Just like the love from You above.
Amen.

Songs

Sing this "piggyback" song from *Little Ones Sing Praise* (CPH), to the melody "Are You Sleeping?"

I am special, I am special.
God sent me, God sent me.

To my mom and daddy, to my mom and daddy.
They love me, they love me.

Books to Read

Celebrate Family, Heidi Bratton, CPH, 2000.

Hush, Little One, Anita Reith Stohs, CPH, 2002.

I Know My Mommy Loves Me, Barbara Wolfgram, CPH, 1999.

The Mother Who Prayed, Leslie Santa Maria, CPH, 2000.

"I Am God's Gift" Pictures

Saying and Showing

Tell this story to the children as a discussion starter about saying versus showing love:

Once upon a time two little rabbits lived in a cozy hole with their mother. On this particular day, Muffy was busy coloring a picture and Fluffy sat in the corner reading a book.

"I love you so much, Momma," said Muffy, "I'm drawing this picture just for you."

"And it's a beautiful picture too," said Momma Bunny. "But don't forget to pick up your crayons when you're done."

Soon Muffy got hungry and went hopping off to Farmer Foster's garden for a little snack. Her crayons still lay all over the floor.

Momma Bunny came into the room. Fluffy was still reading her book. "Where's Muffy?" asked Momma Bunny.

"She went to Farmer Foster's garden to find a snack."

"Oh, no!" said Momma Bunny. "I asked her to pick up her crayons when she was finished drawing."

"I'll pick them up, Momma," said Fluffy. And she did.

Now who do you think showed love for Momma Bunny?

Mother's Day Gifts

Have the children make gifts to give to give their mothers for Mother's Day. For example, ask the children to finish this sentence: "I love my mother because …" Make a list of their answers. Copy the list for each student, then roll it up and tie it with a ribbon. Have the children give it to their mothers.

Bouncing Babies

Assemble items for a learning center about babies. Include a small tub with water where children can wash a plastic baby doll. Have clothes, towels, bottles, diapers, rattles, and other baby items available.

You might wish to invite a mother to bring her baby to class. If possible, ask her to bathe and feed the baby at school.

"I Am God's Gift" Pictures

1. Cut out a simple outline of a child.
2. Write these words on the cutouts: "I am God's gift."
3. Let the children use cotton swabs to paint on the cutout shapes.

MAY

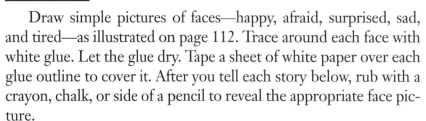

Silly? Sad? Surprised?

Bible references: Jeremiah 31:3;
Romans 8:35–39

PREPARATION

Draw simple pictures of faces—happy, afraid, surprised, sad, and tired—as illustrated on page 112. Trace around each face with white glue. Let the glue dry. Tape a sheet of white paper over each glue outline to cover it. After you tell each story below, rub with a crayon, chalk, or side of a pencil to reveal the appropriate face picture.

Materials Needed

White glue

White paper

Crayon, chalk, or pencil

DEVOTION

One morning Benji rushed outside to play. The sun shone. The birds sang. He jumped on his bicycle and started pedaling. He pedaled faster and faster. The trees flashed past. The wind blew his hair. Benji loved to ride his bike. How do you think he felt? *Make a rubbing of the happy face and show it to the class.* That's right. Benji felt happy.

A little later Benji got off his bike. He started to play in his sandbox. Lots of flowers grew right next to his sandbox. Benji liked to smell them. They smelled so-o-o good. Benji put down his shovel and leaned over to smell a bright red flower. Just then he heard a buzzing sound. A big bumblebee headed right toward him. How do you think he felt now? *Make a rubbing of the afraid face and show it to the children.* Benji was afraid. He didn't want the bumblebee to sting him. But the bumblebee flew right past Benji and disappeared into the flowerbed. That made Benji feel much better.

Benji loved to eat. His favorite foods were cookies, pizza, and juicy apples. He went inside the house. "I'm hungry," he told his mother.

"I thought you might want something to eat after all that playing," his mother said. "So I made a special snack for you. Close you eyes and hold out your hand," she said.

Benji closed his eyes tightly and stretched out his hand. He felt his mother place something warm and round in his hand. "I know what it is!" he said. "It's a chocolate chip cookie!" *Make a rubbing* of the surprised face and show it to the children. Benji felt surprised. He didn't know his mother was baking his favorite snack.

After finishing another cookie and some cold milk, Benji started to go back outside to play. But when he opened the door, a cold wind blew in. The sunshine had disappeared. Now dark clouds filled the sky, and big drops of rain fell on the ground. *Make a rubbing of the sad face and show it to the class.* This is how Benji's face looked now. He was sad.

So Benji got out his puzzles and trains and blocks, and he listened to the rain as it fell on the roof. Pretty soon Benji rubbed his eyes. He didn't want to take a nap, but today his eyes felt so heavy. *Make a rubbing of the tired face and show it to the children.* Benji closed his eyes and curled up on the floor and fell asleep.

It's not even lunchtime yet, but Benji has already had so many feelings. He's felt *(point to each rubbing as you mention that emotion)* happy, afraid, surprised, sad, and tired.

Each day we all feel many different ways. We might feel silly one minute and bossy the next. And then a little later we might feel lonely or excited or scared.

No matter how we feel, Jesus always loves us. He loves us when we're glad or mad, good or bad. He loves us when we're awake or tired, silly or serious, happy or sad. Jesus loves us all the time.

Let the children join you in the following motion poem. After each verse, repeat the refrain.

Sometimes I'm as angry as a buzzing bee.
(Move hand like bee in flight.)
Refrain: But all the time, all the time, Jesus loves me.
(Hug self.)
Sometimes I'm silly as a monkey in a tree.
(Scratch head and make a silly face.)
Refrain
Sometimes I won't eat even one green pea.

(Cross arms on chest and shake head no.)
Refrain
Sometimes I trip and fall and scrape my knee.
(Rub knee.)
Refrain
Sometimes I wish I could sail across the sea.
(Put hand to brow and look toward the distance.)
Refrain
Sometimes I scream louder than the TV.
(Cup hands around mouth.)
Refrain
Sometimes I'm sad, as sad as I can be.
(Rub eyes with fist.)
Refrain
Sometimes I run and jump and feel so free.
(Run and jump in place.)

Prayer

Dear Jesus, sometimes I feel so many different ways that I get confused. Thank You for loving me all the time, no matter how I feel. Amen.

Songs

Sing these songs from *Little Ones Sing Praise* by CPH:

"If You Feel Happy"

"When I'm Feeling Scared Or Sad"

Books to Read

ABC Book of Feelings, Marlys and Joe Boddy, CPH, 1991.

Celebrate Feelings, Heidi Bratton, CPH, 2000.

Sheep Care, Anne Catharine Blake, CPH, 1998.

Sheep Share, Anne Catharine Blake, CPH, 2001.

MAY

Move to the Music

1. Give each child a scarf or crepe paper streamer.

2. Play music of different types and tempos.

3. Let children move and dance as the music makes them feel.

Puppet Talk

1. Construct a simple puppet theater. You might just drape a sheet over two chairs and have the children sit behind the sheet while their puppets talk above it.

2. Place several puppets in the theater and let the children make them talk.

How Does This Child Feel?

Show pictures of children expressing an emotion. After you show each picture ask, "How does this child feel? What do you think happened to make him or her feel that way?"

Face Pictures

Happy

Surprised

Sad

Tired

Afraid

Bandages from Heaven

Bible references: Matthew 8:1–3; Mark 1:30–31; 10:46–52; Luke 5:17–26; John 4:46–53

PREPARATION

Materials Needed

Floppy rag doll with bandage on the knee

DEVOTION

Hold up rag doll. This is Sarabeth. She doesn't feel well today. When she woke up this morning, her nose was all stuffy. And then, when she was getting ready for school, she fell and scraped her knee. Poor Sarabeth. But her mother gave her a big hug and put this bandage on Sarabeth's knee. I think she feels a little better now.

Did you ever have a morning like Sarabeth's? *Let children tell their stories.* I suppose now and then we all have a morning like that. Your tummy is sick or your toe hurts or your head feels stuffy and hot. Those aren't very enjoyable mornings. We feel like staying in bed.

Sometimes staying in bed is just what we need to feel better. Other times some juice and good food help us to feel better. And now and then we need to go to the doctor's office or the drug store for some medicine. All these things help us feel better when we're sick or hurt.

God gives us all these helpers to take care of us when we don't feel well. He gives us bandages and doctors and medicine. He gives us hospitals and nurses and hugs from Mom and Dad.

God wants us to pray to Him all the time. That means even when we are sick or hurt. God wants to help us. He wants to be with us. He wants to heal all our hurts.

The Bible tells about many times when Jesus healed people. One man had sores on his skin. Jesus just touched him, and the man's sores were gone! One woman was lying in bed sick with a fever. Jesus took her hand, helped her up, and her fever was gone. She felt so well that she started to cook dinner. One blind man sat by the side of the road. Jesus made him see again! That happy man could see blue sky and green grass and Jesus smiling at him.

One time four men had a friend who couldn't walk. They couldn't get close to Jesus because of all the people around Him. So they cut a hole in the roof of the building and lowered their

MAY

113

friend down right in front of Jesus. The man who couldn't walk loved Jesus so much. Jesus told him, "Get up, pick up your bed, and go home." And the man did. He could walk and run and jump all the way home.

Another time a little boy was very sick. His mother and father were so worried about him. The father hurried to find Jesus. "My little boy is so sick," the man said to Jesus. "Please help him."

"Go home," Jesus said. "Your little boy is well." And he was! The little boy got better at the same time Jesus said this to the father. Jesus helped the little boy without even going to see him.

Jesus wants to help you when you are sick or hurt too. You can pray to Jesus and ask Him to help you. He will always listen, and He will always help. Jesus loves you so much!

Prayer

Say a special prayer asking Jesus to help someone who is sick. Be sure to pray for any children in your class who are absent because of illness. Also let the children tell you about people in their lives who are sick and need prayers.

Songs

Sing these songs from *Little Ones Sing Praise* by CPH:

"He's God the Whole World in His Hands"

"Jesus, You Help"

"Jesus, What a Name"

Book to Read

When Will I Get Better?, Robin Prince Monroe, CPH, 1998.

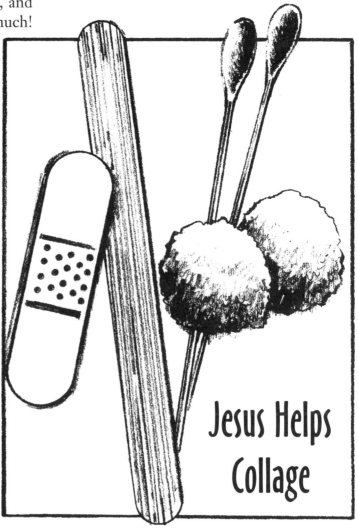

Jesus Helps Collage

God's Loving Care Motion Poem

Encourage the children to join you in the following motion poem.

Sometimes I'm sick—as sick as can be.

(Place hands over stomach.)

It might be my head or even my knee.

(Touch head, then knee.)

Then I fold my hands and say a prayer.

(Fold hands.)

I know God above will always care.

(Hug self.)

God gives us bandages and medicine too.

(Nod head yes.)

Doctors and nurses for me and for you.

(Point to self, then others.)

From my tiptoes up to my shiny hair,

(Stand on tiptoes and place hand on top of head.)

Thank You, dear God, for Your loving care!

(Clap hands.)

Jesus Helps Collage

Assemble items associated with health care and let the children make collages. You might include bits of gauze, bandages, cotton balls, tongue depressors, tissues, and cotton swabs. Write "Jesus Helps" at the top of each collage.

Hospital Tour

Arrange for the children to tour a nearby hospital. Many hospitals offer special tours for young children. If such a tour is not available in your area, you can still visit the hospital's public areas. Many children never see the inside of a hospital unless they are seriously ill or injured or until someone they love disappears into the large building. As you visit, point out that God cares for us through doctors and nurses.

Healthy Snacks

Have the children help you prepare a healthy snack. Reinforce the idea that God gives us good food to help our bodies grow and to keep us healthy. Following are some suggestions:

Banana slices on thin pretzel sticks

Celery sticks filled with peanut butter and topped with raisins

Peanut butter on apple slices

Cheese cubes

Applesauce sprinkled with cinnamon

Mix of raisins, peanuts, and a few chocolate chips

MAY
✳

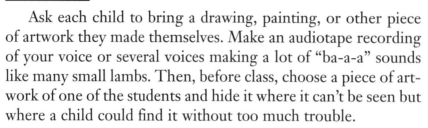

Little Lambs

Bible references: Matthew 18:12–14;
Luke 12:7; John 10:3

PREPARATION

Ask each child to bring a drawing, painting, or other piece of artwork they made themselves. Make an audiotape recording of your voice or several voices making a lot of "ba-a-a" sounds like many small lambs. Then, before class, choose a piece of artwork of one of the students and hide it where it can't be seen but where a child could find it without too much trouble.

Materials Needed

Drawing or other piece of artwork from each child in the class

Tape player and tape you made

DEVOTION

Look what I have today! I have some beautiful pieces of art. *Hold up several drawings.* This art was made by all of you. I have one piece of art from each boy and girl in our class. I think these pieces of art are special. They are special because you made them and each of you is special to me. I have art from … *(Hold up each drawing and name child who created it. All children should be named except the one whose art is hidden.)*

Oh no! Where is *(name of child whose art is hidden)*'s piece of art? I know it was here! It was an especially beautiful piece, too. We just have to find it! Will you boys and girls help me find *(child's name)*'s artwork? Let's look around our classroom. I know we can find it if we look hard.

Let children hunt around classroom for the missing piece of art. After it is found say, Thank you! I'm so glad you found *(child's name)*'s artwork. *(Child's name)* is special to me, and *(his or her)* piece of art is special, too. *(Child's name)*, will you come up here and sit next to me while I tell a story from the Bible about something else that was missing?

A man had 100 sheep. *Play tape with "baa" sounds.* That's a lot of sheep! The man was a shepherd. A shepherd is a person who takes care of sheep. This shepherd took very good care of his sheep. Each day he led them to green fields and hills where they could munch grass and drink cool water. If any bears or lions tried to hurt the sheep, the shepherd would protect them.

One day the shepherd watched his sheep eating the green grass. "These sheep are so special to me," he thought. "Look at

JUNE

Curly jumping right over Oatmeal. And that silly Pinkie is chasing Woolie all over the field." The shepherd looked at all his sheep. Each one had a name of its own. The shepherd said, "There's Big Foot and there's Little One and there's Black Eyes and … oh no! Where's Tiny Toes? I can't find Tiny Toes!" *Turn off tape player.*

The shepherd looked and looked. But Tiny Toes was nowhere to be found. The shepherd was so worried. He left all his other sheep and climbed up the hills looking for Tiny Toes. He looked under trees and inside caves and behind rocks. But he couldn't find Tiny Toes.

Finally, the shepherd heard a soft "baa." *Turn tape player back on.* He lifted a low branch and there lay Tiny Toes. The shepherd lifted the sheep into his arms, scratched her fuzzy head, and gave her a hug. "I'm so glad I found you, Tiny Toes," he said. "You are so special to me." *Turn off tape player.*

Jesus is our Shepherd, and we are His little lambs. He loves us and cares for us just like the shepherd in our story. He knows all of our names. The Bible tells us He even knows how many hairs are on our head. Each of you is so special to Jesus. He loves you more than anything.

Prayer

Dear Jesus, we are so happy that we are Your special little lambs. Thank You for loving us just like a shepherd loves his sheep. Amen.

Songs

"Jesus Loves the Little Ones Like Me," *Little Ones Sing Praise,* CPH.

"A Little Woolly Lamb," *The Little Christian's Songbook,* CPH.

Or try this "piggyback" song to the melody "Mary Had a Little Lamb."

Jesus loves me oh so much, oh so much, oh so much.
Jesus loves me oh so much,
He even knows my name.
Repeat first two lines but add one of the following as the third line.
He's by my side each day.
And He loves each of you.
And I love Jesus, too.

Books to Read

Beatrice Loses Her Doll, Pam Halter, CPH, 2001.

Sheep Lost, Anne Catharine Blake, CPH, 1998.

The Shepherd and the Lost Sheep, Allia Zobel-Nolan, CPH, 2000.

The Good Shepherd, Joan Bader, CPH, 1998.

JUNE

Missing Numbers

1. Write each numeral from 1 to 10 on index cards. If desired, add stickers or circles on each card to match the numeral on that card.

2. Take one card out. Arrange the remaining cards in order from 1 to 10. Ask what number is missing.

3. Add the missing card.

4. Repeat as often as the children remain interested, each time removing a different numeral card.

Lamb Bits

1. Copy the lamb outline shown here and make one lamb for each child.

2. Let the children cut out the lamb and glue on Styrofoam bits or pieces of cotton balls.

3. After using the lambs for the lamb hunt below, make a bulletin board display by placing them on a green paper "grass" background under the title "Jesus' Little Lambs."

Lamb Hunt

1. Hide the lamb outlines around the classroom.

2. Let the children hunt for them. If any are not easily found, hunt harder until they are found.

3. Remind the children that every lamb is special, just like every child is special to Jesus.

Lamb Bits Pattern

JUNE

118

All Kinds of Families

Bible reference: Exodus 20:12

PREPARATION

Materials Needed

At least 10 small dolls, both male and female, that can be grouped and regrouped to form various family units. If you prefer, make spoon puppets. Use markers to draw faces and hair on plastic spoons. Set each spoon handle into a small lump of clay so it will stand alone.

Bible storybook showing pictures of some of the families mentioned in the devotion.

DEVOTION

God gives us families to love us and take care of us. It feels good to be part of a family. People in a family do many things for one another. They help one another and share with one another and pray for one another.

Place all the dolls where children can see them. Families come in all shapes and sizes. Some families are big. They have lots and lots of people in them just like this. *Point to dolls.* Other families are small. Sometimes one person lives all alone. *Hold up one doll.* Other families have just two people in them. *Hold up two dolls.* Some families have one child. *Separate three dolls from the others.* Or two children. *Add another doll.* Or three children. *Add another doll.* Some families have a grandmother or grandfather living with them. *Add one or two more dolls.*

The size of your family doesn't matter. All that matters is that you love your family and your family loves you. That's what makes families special.

Show pictures from a Bible storybook as you mention each of the following families.

The Bible tells us about many families.

Adam and Eve, and their children Cain and Abel, were the first family God made.

Noah and his family lived in a big boat with lots and lots of animals.

Abraham and Sarah were very old when their son, Isaac, was born.

Jacob and Esau were brothers. One time they had a big fight. But they forgave each other.

Joseph had 11 brothers. Now that's a big family!

Moses' mother tried to hide him from a mean king. But a kind princess found him and became his foster mother.

JUNE

Timothy's mother and grandmother read stories from the Bible to him. He liked to learn about God's love.

David was the youngest in his family. But he became a king!

Even Jesus had a family. He must have helped Joseph work in the carpenter shop. And I'm sure He helped Mary do things like carry water to their house.

God has been making families for a long, long time. We would be hungry without our families to cook for us. And we would be sad without our families to read books to us and take us to the playground to play. But most of all, we would be lonely without our families to love us. Let's thank God for our families. *(Say prayer below.)*

Prayer

Dear God, thank You for Mom and Daddy too.
For sisters, brothers, and babies so new.
For cousins and aunts and uncles so tall,
For Grandma and Grandpa. I love them all.
Oh thank You, dear God, for my family.
Thank You for giving them all to me. Amen.

Songs

"In My Family," *The Little Christian's Songbook*, CPH.

"Love, Love, Love," *Little Ones Sing Praise*, CPH.

Books to Read

Adopted and Loved Forever, Annetta E. Dellinger, CPH, 1987.

Celebrate Family, Heidi Bratton, CPH, 2000.

Daddy Promises, Kerry Arquette, CPH, 1999.

I Have a New Family Now, Robin Prince Monroe, CPH 1998.

JUNE

Family Houses and a Neighborhood

1. Cut construction paper into large simple house shapes.

2. Let the children look through old catalogs and cut out pictures representing each of the people in their families.

3. Glue the pictures onto the construction paper house.

4. As each child identifies the members of his or her family, write their names above the appropriate pictures.

5. Assemble the family houses on a bulletin board marked with street names to form a neighborhood map.

How Many in Your Family?

1. Send each child home with a plastic sandwich bag filled with 10 jellybeans, candy-coated chocolate pieces, or cereal pieces.

2. Include a short note asking a family member to help the child count how many persons are in their family and leave one candy or cereal piece in the bag for each person. The child may eat the rest.

3. Ask children to bring the bag back to class the next day and count and compare family sizes.

Father's Day Gifts

1. Ask each child to bring in a smooth rock to use as a paperweight. Set out several colors of tempera paints and let each child paint his or her rock. After the paint has dried, shellac the rocks to protect them and make them shine. Glue pieces of felt to the bottom of the painted rocks. Have each child give the paperweight to Dad, Grandpa, or another adult.

2. Ask each child to bring in a man's handkerchief. Let the children decorate the handkerchiefs with permanent markers. (Be sure to cover their clothing with paint smocks.) Write each child's name on his or her handkerchief under these words, "I love you." Wrap in tissue paper decorated with sponge prints or stickers.

House Construction

Let the children build houses from craft sticks, boxes, blocks, construction paper squares, or play dough. Encourage housekeeping activities. Add some additional props to your housekeeping center: hats, old sheets to make tents or houses, pitchers and bowls to pour water, etc.

JUNE

PREPARATION

Materials Needed

One puppet

DEVOTION

Teacher: Good morning, Miranda.

Miranda: *(head hanging sadly)* What's so good about it?

Teacher: *(surprised)* Well … let's see … this morning I had French toast for breakfast. That's one good thing. French toast is my favorite breakfast food.

Miranda: *(starts to cry)* I don't want to talk about breakfast.

Teacher: What's wrong, Miranda?

Miranda: Everything! First, I spilled my milk all over the floor. Then my baby sister broke my new toy. Then my mother made me wear a scratchy sweater. Then I pinched my finger. And then Theodore made a face at me when I got to school.

Teacher: Sounds like you have had a lot of problems this morning.

Miranda: That's for sure. This is a terrible, awful, horrible day!

Teacher: It's not much fun when a day starts out like yours did. But isn't there something you're forgetting, Miranda?

Miranda: What's that?

Teacher: Today is the day God has made. He wants you to be happy and to enjoy His wonderful day.

Miranda: It's hard to enjoy a day like the one I'm having.

Teacher: Oh, I don't know. Look around. All your friends are smiling at you. The birds are singing. The green grass is growing and growing. Bright flowers are blooming. That seems like a pretty good day to me.

Miranda: *(looks around)* I guess you're right. I was so upset that I missed all those good things.

Teacher: Sometimes that happens. When it does, just stop and look around at the wonderful day God has created. And remember that Jesus loves you. He's with you no matter what kind of day you're having. That should put the joy back in your heart.

JUNE

Miranda: *(happy again)* You're right! I feel much happier. Thank You, Jesus! Thank You for this wonderful day!

Close by singing one of the praise songs suggested below.

Prayer

Thank You, God, for this wonderful day!
I've so many things I want to say.
Hallelujah!
Praise the Lord!
Rejoice! Rejoice!
God is great!
Amen.

Songs

The following songs are from *Little Ones Sing Praise* by CPH:
"Rejoice in the Lord Always"
"This Is the Day"
"Hallelujah! Praise Ye the Lord!"
"Happy All the Time"
"I Have the Joy"

Happy Hearts Pattern

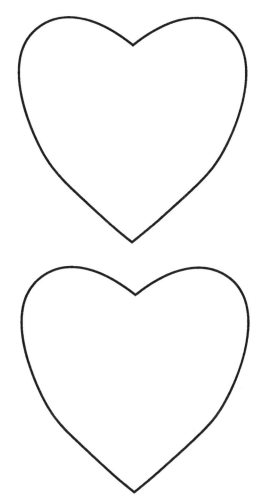

123

Stencil Hearts

Try this project outdoors on a day when there is no breeze:

1. Cut a large heart from cardboard or heavy paper.

2. Cover the grass or sidewalk with newspaper.

3. Tape the cutout heart to the center of the newspaper.

4. Fill a spray bottle with thinned tempera paint.

5. Let the children spray around the stencil heart.

6. When they are finished, remove the heart and let dry.

Happy Hearts

1. Cut out construction-paper hearts.

2. Let each child decorate a heart with a happy face. Glue on a rickrack smile, button eyes and nose, and curling-ribbon hair.

3. Display on a bulletin board under the heading "Jesus Is My Joy."

Mini Rejoice Posters

1. Write "Rejoice" or "God Is Great" or "Hallelujah" or "Praise the Lord" on 3" × 5" or 4" × 6" index cards. Give each child a card.

2. Let the children decorate the cards with a "happy day" picture.

3. Let them glue a tongue depressor to the back of each card as a handle.

JUNE

PREPARATION

Place a small cross in box or wrap it in plain brown paper and hide it outside. Make a simple picture map the children can use to help them find the "hidden treasure." Place an X on the map to show where the treasure is hidden.

Materials Needed

Small cross

Treasure map you have made

DEVOTION

A treasure is something that is very important to us. We all have many different treasures. I have an old coin my grandfather gave to me a long time ago. That coin is very special to me. It's one of my treasures. What are some of your treasures? *Let the children tell about their treasures.*

Today we're going on a treasure hunt. We're going to use this map *(hold up map)* to hunt outside for a hidden treasure. If you look carefully at this map, you will find clues that tell us where the treasure is hidden. *Gather children around the map. Help them identify objects on the map to obtain clues about where the treasure is hidden—for example, a big oak tree, a picnic bench, a fence, etc.* Let's take this map with us and hunt outside for the hidden treasure.

After the children have found the hidden treasure, bring them together to finish the devotion. I'm so glad we found the hidden treasure. Let's open it and find out what it is. Look! It's a cross. That's a wonderful treasure, isn't it? The cross reminds us of Jesus. He died on the cross to save us from all our sins, and then He became alive again. And Jesus promises to take us to heaven someday. I think that's the best treasure we could have possibly found. Jesus is the greatest treasure of all.

This summer, when you are at home playing with all your toys, or going down the slide at the playground, or building sand castles at the beach, or going to church, or having fun at vacation Bible school, remember Jesus. He is right there with you all the time. He is your best Friend. Jesus loves you and cares for you all the time. Jesus is our best, our greatest, our most wonderful treasure.

Prayer

At home or away, at school or at play, be with me, Jesus. I can be happy all the time because of You, Jesus. You are my greatest treasure of all. Amen.

Songs

While the children are gathered together outside, you might like to have a praise celebration and sing many of the Jesus songs the children have enjoyed this past year. The songs suggested below are from *Little Ones Sing Praise* by CPH:

"Go Tell"

"Jesus Loves the Little Children"

"Jesus! What a Name"

"Let Us Sing for Joy"

Books to Read

Bible Friends: Who's Hiding?, Sally Lloyd Jones, CPH, 2001.

The Hidden Prince, Jeffrey E. Burkart, CPH, 2002.

Why I Love You, God, Michelle Medlock Adams, CPH, 2002.

Jesus! What a Name

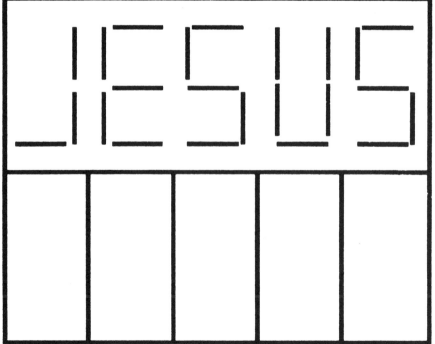

Treasure Box

1. Ask each child to bring one treasure from home.

2. As the children arrive for the day, ask them to place their treasures into a special box somewhere in the classroom. Also place a cross or picture of Jesus inside the box.

3. At an appropriate time, let each child share his or her treasure with the others.

4. After all treasures have been shared, show the cross or picture of Jesus. Stress that Jesus is our greatest treasure.

Trail Mix

1. Let the children mix together as desired: granola cereal, raisins, chocolate chips, and peanuts.

2. Put equal amounts of trail mix into sandwich bags.

3. Let the children enjoy their trail mix after the treasure hunt activity.

Jesus! What a Name

1. Cut a sheet of poster board to measure approximately 22" x 15". Divide the poster board in half horizontally.

2. At the top of the poster board use 23 toothpicks to spell out "J E S U S" (see illustration).

3. Glue the toothpicks to the poster board. Place the poster board on a table next to a pile of toothpicks.

4. Let the children take turns arranging the loose toothpicks beneath those glued down to duplicate "J E S U S."

Remember Jesus

Have children make a simple wall hanging to help them remember Jesus this summer:

1. Cut construction-paper circles to fit inside the plastic lids from one-pound coffee cans or margarine tubs, and glue them down.

2. Paste a picture of Jesus in the center of the circle.

3. Use a marker to write these words around the picture of Jesus: "My Greatest Treasure—Jesus."

4. Punch a hole in the top and thread yarn through the hole.

5. Encourage the children to hang the pictures at home to remind them about Jesus throughout the summer.

JUNE

Love in a Box

Shirley K. Morgenthaler

Shirley K. Morgenthaler